MW01006412

Fatal Friendship

A true crime account as told by
Allen Roberts, Esther Roberts, and others

With Beecher Smith

ISBN 0-7414-3459-8

Transcript of the August 11, 1992, WMC-TV Channel 5 Broadcast and the news articles from *The Commercial Appeal* are copyrighted properties of those respective entities and are reproduced herein with their express permission.

There were 49 articles in *The Commercial Appeal* pertaining to the Doe Roberts case and those involved in it. The eight we felt most germane are reproduced verbatim herein.

Published by:

PUBLISHING.COM

1094 New DeHaven Street, Suite 100
West Conshohocken, PA 19428-2713
Info@buybooksontheweb.com
www.buybooksontheweb.com
Toll-free (877) BUY BOOK
Local Phone (610) 941-9999
Fax (610) 941-9959

Printed in the United States of America

Printed on Recycled Paper

Published August 2007

DEDICATION

This book is dedicated to the memory of
Martha Eudora Jones ("Doe") Roberts
and all who loved her.

FOREWORD

This book is the product of the dedication and love of Esther Roberts for her husband Allen Roberts and the thirteen month ordeal he faced when Doe, his wife of 44 years, was kidnapped in August of 1992, with her body not being found, and the case not being solved, until over a year later. To bring this to publication, she engaged professional journalists to interview the many individuals involved first hand in this true crime account.

Except for "The Perpetrator," whose words, although not authentic, were reconstructed from his confessions and inserted as vignettes among the accounts of his victims to reflect his thought processes contemporaneously as they reveal theirs, all accounts herein are transcribed from interviews made with the interviewees' express consent or from official transcripts of court records. Because of legal issues which arose after this book was substantially completed, some individuals' accounts had to be revised or deleted and the account of Allen Roberts, and sometimes an omniscient third person narrator substituted to protect First Amendment rights of the authors.

The crimes mentioned herein deeply affected an entire community. The accounts of those others who suffered along with Allen Roberts lend a solemn credence to his chronicle.

Beecher Smith

May 22, 2007

Doe Roberts, shortly before she was kidnapped in 1992.

The Eads United Methodist Church in 2006.

Allen and Doe Roberts at a Square Dancing event in 1988.

Esther Hammons in 1986.

Esther and Allen Roberts at the
Mid-South Square Dancing Festival in November of 1994.

Esther and Allen Roberts on their honeymoon
in May of 1994.

CHAPTER ONE

On Tuesday morning, August 11, 1992, anchorman Joe Birch of WMC-TV, Channel 5, Memphis, Tennessee, conducted the videotaping of the following broadcast which aired on that evening's news:

"My name is Allen Roberts. My wife is Doe Roberts. We have been married for 44 years. We have no children, and my wife is my life.

"This past Friday morning, my wife, Doe Roberts, was abducted from our home. I have not been able to obtain her release. I have no way to communicate with whoever is holding her; therefore, I am asking the news media to broadcast this plea.

"I make this plea for mercy and compassion from whoever is holding Doe to consider her medical condition. Doe has severe asthma and if she doesn't receive daily medication, her life is in danger.

"I appeal for Doe's release so that she can receive the necessary medical treatment that can save her life. If Doe is released unharmed, I will meet any demand. I will do whatever is necessary to obtain Doe's release."

(WMC, Channel 5, Six O'clock News,
Tuesday, August 11, 1992.)

Allen Roberts

With this statement I made public the nightmare that had begun four days earlier. Nothing in life prepared me for that terrible day. None of the lessons I had learned in business, college, or the Merchant Marines applied to this emergency. Nothing would ever again be the same, and I have been

1

forever changed.

I pray that as you read these words, you never have to say, "I know just how you feel." I thank you for reading this far. Just thinking that my story might touch the life of another encouraged me to write this.

Our search for my wife led me, my family, friends, the investigators, and even the media on a long and tortured path before the truth was discovered. Most true crime books are told through the eyes of the investigators—how they uncover leads, the drama behind the scenes, planning strategy, and details. However interesting such cases may be, this was not a "case" to me. This was my wife. If you are a member of the law enforcement community, regard this as a primer—this is how it feels on the other side of an investigation.

The FBI put all our lives under a magnifying glass. During the investigation, I was not made privy to crucial information. What they had been told by people, friends, and even my family, was not shared with me until after the case was solved.

The events of that awful year didn't just happen to Doe and me—they were shared by our entire community. My story is like a war that was fought on several fronts—in our home, within the town of Eads, among our square dance friends, and in our church.

A serpent lay coiled in our midst, ready to strike, but we did not know it. After putting this book together, we now see clearly important pieces of the puzzle that none of us recognized at the time.

* * *

During the first week of August 1992, I felt no sense of foreboding. Doe and I led active lives, pursuing business, church and civic interests, both together and independently. We were literally in the prime of our lives, having struggled and sacrificed in our early years. We had built a sizeable estate together and were enjoying the comforts of financial security. Apart from Doe's asthma, we were both healthy.

In the wider world, our first President Bush was concerned with atrocities in the detention camps in Bosnia and was running "war games" in Kuwait. There was absolutely no concern at the Summer Olympics about the Dream Team in Barcelona, Spain—Charles Barkley, Magic Johnson, and their teammates were going to mop the floor with the other basketball teams. Carl Lewis would shove his age down the judges' throats and win his third gold medal in the long jump. In Memphis, Tennessee, folks were watching our own Olympic track star, Rochelle Stevens.

Memphians were gearing up for the onslaught of Elvis fans for the annual candlelight vigil at Graceland. A Shelby County general election was drawing to a close. The most hotly contested seat had been that for the office of County Assessor. White Republican Harold Sterling beat out incumbent black Democrat Michael Hooks by a narrow margin. Memphis's first elected black mayor, Dr. W. W. Herenton, was being criticized for his campaign endorsement supporting Hooks that was placed only on black radio stations.

If politics and sports were normal, the weather was bizarre. August in Shelby County is like the Mississippi River itself—moving slowly in the weight of the heat, but that first week the temperature high suddenly dropped to 75 degrees. No one could remember such a cool temperature for that time of year. Doe loved it and used it as an opportunity to get in more gardening. She worked in her wildflower bed in the front of our house. The wildflowers were sheltered in the shade of oaks and dogwoods that lined the road. Doe also enjoyed working in our vegetable garden behind the house, producing home-grown tomatoes and turnip greens.

We lived in the small community of Eads, Tennessee. We had bought the site for our home place, some 150 acres, during the Seventies, but we didn't build the house until several years later.

Eads lies twenty-five miles east of Memphis, Tennessee, on the eastern border of Shelby County and the western border of Fayette County. Shelby County is the southwestern most county of the state. The county's western boundary is the Mississippi River, with Arkansas on the other side. Mississippi's state line is the southern boundary. The city of Memphis comprises much of the county.

It has been said that the Mississippi Delta starts in the lobby of the Peabody Hotel. Unlike the flat lands to the south, Memphis sits on high bluffs, overlooking the river. Going east, gentle hills begin, though these are not readily apparent in the density of the city. Beyond the city limits, the hills become steeper, more pronounced. The area is threaded together by two-lane blacktop roads that curve and sweep under trees arching from either side. In the summer, when you drive eastward from Memphis, you feel the temperature drop as you leave the main roads, and you breathe in clean country air fragrant with freshly cut grass. Homes are scattered, a patchwork of both upscale and modest.

Eads is a small, unincorporated community. There's a post office, but no mayor nor government of any kind, not even a constable. The U.S. Post Office is the only official government building in the entire community. In 1992 there were less than 300 registered voters. The center of the community is a grassy rectangle that had once been a railroad easement. Some years before, Doe put feet to her dream of a place where the community could get together. At her urging, I worked to have the easement ceded to the township. Then we built the Civic Club, a large, log structure which sits on a corner near the small post office. The Civic Club building lends itself to many different activities, including the weekly meeting of our square dance club.

Jefferson Road is on the east side of the Civic Center. Drive north for a few moments on Jefferson and you come to our church, Eads United Methodist.

It is important to focus on this church because it is where the evil that came upon us originated, then stretched out and ensnared most of the members. Doe and I had belonged to that church since the early Eighties. We were Presbyterians before we moved out to Eads, but truth is, you don't join the denomination, you join a particular congregation. When we visited Eads Methodist our first Sunday, we sensed the warmth and spiritual love of the members who made us feel at home immediately, so we decided to stay, join, and worship there.

I can see clearly in my mind's eye how it was on Sunday mornings. The sanctuary is small, more of a chapel, arrayed in Wesleyan simplicity, yet comfortable and inviting. Stained glass windows line the side walls. The geometric design of each window is the same: a slender white cross with a crimson square in the center bordered at the top with an arch of small green panes.

The pulpit is on a slightly raised, recessed dais. This space is an alcove formed by a vestibule on the right and a storage room on the left. A more elaborate stained glass window is the centerpiece behind the oak pulpit. A short divided communion rail of light oak separates the dais from the pews. An altar table stands directly in front of the pulpit carved with the words, "This do in remembrance of me." The carpet is dark red; the pew cushions match the green in the windows.

The church seats about 80, which was the size of the congregation when we joined. By August 1992, however, for a number of reasons, our numbers had dwindled.

Doe rarely missed a Sunday. My attendance was less regular, but like Doe, my support was wholehearted.

The church faces Jefferson Road. Behind the church is an

asphalt parking lot I had graded and paved myself. When the land was purchased, hopes were high that future growth would require a large plot. As yet, this need hasn't arisen, so the land beyond the parking lot remains covered in trees and wildflowers. The church is "U" shaped, with the sanctuary and a tiny children's nursery forming one side of the U and the kitchen the other. No offices.

Connecting these areas is the long, narrow recreation hall. A utilitarian space, the walls are covered with tongue-in-groove pine paneling with dark linoleum tiles on the floor. Folding tables running down the middle of the room stay set-up most of the time. Accordion dividers allow the room to be separated into three sections for Sunday school. Near the short steps leading up to the sanctuary is a small table for the coffee pot. After Sunday school, the usual twenty-five or thirty who come for church gather in small groups, cups in hand, to visit.

I can still see Doe standing there. At age 65, my wife was about five feet, five inches tall, with short gray hair combed in bangs across her forehead. She kept her figure trim and attractive by working in our garden, taking aerobics, and square dancing. She frequently flashed her wide smile, which softened the strong line of high cheek bones she inherited from a Native American ancestor. Doe's movements were brisk. She would enter the recreation hall brushing her hands together quickly in her habitual gesture of anticipation—hands so used to giving and helping others—looking forward to the fellowship. With a big smile, she would greet her many friends in the congregation.

People tended to sit in the same pews Sunday after Sunday. Doe and I sat toward the back with our friend Brenda Williamson. Brenda was an attractive blonde in her late thirties who was one of Doe's closest friends, despite their age difference. Brenda's husband, Will, was a fireman and not often in church. On Sundays when Will and I were not there, Doe and Brenda would always sit together in the same pew.

On Monday morning, the week of that fateful Friday, Doe called Brenda, who was also our neighbor, to get a ride to the doctor. I am not sure why Doe didn't ask me to take her that morning. I guess there are times when a woman just wants to spend time with a woman friend.

Doe had curtailed her driving due to recent cataract surgery. She made short trips around Eads, but the drive into Memphis would not have been sensible. Brenda normally would have been happy to do anything Doe wanted. They saw each other or talked almost every day. Doe asked Brenda to take her to a doctor's office an hour away in downtown Memphis, but Brenda's own schedule didn't allow her enough time and she apologetically said she couldn't.

Another reason Brenda begged off was that she couldn't drive the stick shift on Doe's '86 Volkswagen, and her own van was full of construction debris from the shop. A few weeks before, Doe had an asthma attack so severe I had to rush her to the hospital. She fully recovered, but we almost lost her that night. The doctors insisted on monitoring her with regular follow-up office visits.

Doe called Brenda back and said she couldn't find anyone else to take her. She assured Brenda that she could tolerate the debris in the van. Brenda relented, and they spent the day together.

Brenda had been making silk flower arrangements and traveling to crafts fairs to sell them. Doe had repeatedly urged her younger friend to get off the road and open a local shop. My wife was the type of person who encouraged people to do more than they might think they could. She delighted in watching them stretch to better themselves. Brenda had taken Doe's advice at last, and her new gift shop would open the following week at a new mall in Jackson, about 50 miles away. She and her husband had worked all weekend to get ready for the opening day of business.

Brenda told me she remembered that during the drive Doe had church matters on her mind. She asked Brenda if she knew the Chairman of Finance, Charles Lord, had moved some church bank accounts. Charles had recently retired as comptroller at the Defense Depot in Memphis. Most in the congregation appreciated his expertise, but the restraints he put on spending sometimes sparked criticism. Charles and Brenda had often disagreed strongly about expenditures for the young people. Brenda wanted funds for special activities because she felt those would attract more families with children to the church and help it grow; but Charles held in the reins, saying the money needed to be saved for future building expansion.

Doe also told Brenda during the drive that Charles had talked to us about investing in a beer distributorship in Mexico. Charles had mentioned this to me only in passing one Sunday and, as I had no interest, I didn't pursue it with him. Doe confided in Brenda that she thought this was the reason Charles and Sylvia hadn't spoken to her in church recently.

Brenda was preoccupied at the time over what had happened to her nephew. Two men had recently robbed him on his Pepsi Cola truck route. When he pursued the robbers, they shot him, leaving him paralyzed. Doe recounted a hold-up at the little café we had owned years before. Brenda said Doe was emphatic, from that experience, that the best way to survive was to be calm and do exactly what the robbers said. During the terror that followed, Brenda would lie awake nights and replay the memory of that Monday over and over, wondering and praying that Doe might be successful in choosing the path of nonresistance.

Returning from the drive downtown, Doe and Brenda stopped at the new Kroger grocery store on Highway 64. They took advantage of its delicatessen to have lunch and stretch out their time together. Brenda had a hair appointment at 2:00. When she dropped Doe off at home, Doe hesitated before getting out, saying she might just go on with Brenda to the beauty shop. Brenda, in thinking back, said it was as though Doe didn't want to be alone, like she was apprehensive about something. This sounded so unlike Doe, independent and self-reliant as she was. In the end, Doe got out of the van, saying, "No, go on. Allen will be home before we would get back."

* * *

On Tuesday, my wife went to her Extension Club luncheon with a friend and, that evening, to a Civic Club committee meeting. On Wednesday the high temperatures fell into the low seventies. After working in the garden during the afternoon, Doe drove herself to a meeting at the church, which was only a few minutes from our home.

Some of us in the congregation felt that, with all the new families moving into the area, the church had an opportunity to expand its membership. A committee was formed consisting of Karen and Carl Johnson, our youngest couple; Mike Coward, our newest member; Brother Jim DeBardeleban, our pastor; Charles Lord, and me. The group was to discuss plans and find ways to encourage membership.

Doe believed strongly in the church's future and had started a building fund for a new, larger sanctuary. The weekly contributions by the congregation were mounting up and the fund had grown to several thousand dollars. Doe took care of the weekly deposits herself.

Because of a conflict I had that night, Doe attended the committee meeting in my place. She told me later that evening that, when she came in the back door, the group was already gathered around the long table in the recreation hall.

Karen Johnson told me she remembers Doe talking that

evening about planning to drive into Memphis to vote on Thursday, since she had never moved her registration to Eads. At the close of the meeting, Doe left immediately.

Mike Coward later told me he thought she looked pale and he wondered if her asthma might have been giving her trouble.

* * *

Thursday evening Doe and I went to the Civic Club to dance with the Top Spinners, our square dancing club. Doe loved to dance and, that night she appeared well and enthusiastic. We were not going to stay late because someone had telephoned right before we left home. Doe had taken the call. She told me she had made an appointment with the caller, who wanted to meet with me to write a contract on one of my new houses the next morning.

So, that Thursday night, after we came home from square dancing, we went to bed early. I think about that moment. As Doe and I were readying for bed, it was also the time the Johnson's tucked their children in for the night. Brenda would be working late in her craft room, readying her wares for the next day. For them, our other friends and family members, all of whom loved Doe and me, we would be spending the remaining time awake as our last normal evening.

* * *

Friday the nightmare began.

I've reported the events of that day so many times. I have talked about it to everyone who would listen. The FBI agent in charge of the investigation, Jo Anne Overall, said to me later that I would never make a good law enforcement officer because I repeated everything to everybody. As I originally told the events to her, I tell them to you now.

This drama inevitably begins on that Thursday night, when Doe told me a man from Indiana had called to say he had inspected one of my houses for sale on Orr Road, that he liked it, and wanted to come by at 10 o'clock the next morning to sign a contract. He'd indicated to her that he was sold on the property, but he wanted to deal with me directly because he didn't like dealing with women. Doe added that he had an odd accent and sounded like he might be Oriental. I didn't think any of that was too strange. In real estate, we're used to folks with odd attitudes. What mattered was the sale.

Friday morning, I went to the barn for the Dodge pickup. Our barn is a large metal building about twenty yards south of the house and connected to it by a wide driveway. We kept a dump truck, a small tractor, and a backhoe in it. We built the barn large enough to store these vehicles and as a place to hold square dances. I backed the pickup out of the barn and drove up the driveway towards the gate. As I passed the house, the garage door opened. Doe came out and hollered at me.

I'll never forget how she stood there, just inside the garage door. I stopped and rolled down the window. She said the Indiana man had just called again to confirm the appointment. I merely waved and drove on. No goodbye, no kiss. When I remember that moment, I always think about what I should have done. But I assumed Doe would be there when I came back from the appointment.

I drove to the nearby subdivision and met Brenda Keith at the house on Orr Road where we expected to meet our prospect. Brenda is Doe's niece, the daughter of Doe's brother Leonard, and she worked for me in my residential home building business. She is attractive like Doe, with light brown hair and brown eyes. She is also a hard worker. We noticed that some grass wasn't yet established, and the lawns were starting to erode. We spent the morning working on the landscaping while waiting for my prospect.

By about 12 o'clock, the man still hadn't shown up. This was not unusual. Prospects frequently do not show. Although disappointed, I figured something had come up or he had changed his mind. If he was serious, he'd call me back. If he'd changed his mind, then I'd just wait until another buyer came along.

Brenda and I decided we needed some more hay and sod, so I left to go buy some. I drove directly back to Collierville-Arlington Road, stopping at the sod farm to find the owner of the field. I ordered a full pallet of sod and he promised to have it ready in a couple of hours. I then drove down to Highway 64, picked up two sandwiches for Doe and me, and went home for lunch.

When I arrived at our home, the garage door was open, the house unlocked, but Doe wasn't there. Her cart was sitting at the back door, with mail in its basket. She had been outside when I left, so I had expected her to be there, inside, when I first came back in through the back door.

I walked through the house looking for her, but it didn't dawn on me that anything unusual had happened. I might have called out for her, but I don't remember. I didn't become alarmed because there were no signs of any struggle. Nothing appeared disturbed. There wasn't anything out of place to cause me alarm. This was Eads, Tennessee. Bad things don't happen here.

I ate my sandwich and left hers on the table. I felt sure Doe would find it and eat it when she returned from wherever she had gone.

On my way back to the subdivision, I passed an eighteen wheeler stuck on the shoulder of the road and went to some trouble to help the driver get back on the road with a tow from my pickup. Then, when I went to pick up the sod, the proprietor wasn't there and the attendant minding the place didn't know me. I didn't have money or checkbook on me, so I waited almost an hour for the owner to return and allow me to pick up the sod.

At that point I realized I needed physical activity to work off and channel the delayed feelings of tension and frustration caused by the unnecessary wait at the sod store. Brenda Keith and I spent the rest of that hot afternoon laying sod.

It was about 4 o'clock when I returned home, sweating and tired. As I pulled into the drive, I was surprised to see that the garage door was still up.

I drove the truck back to the barn and walked to the house. Doe never left the door up for that length of time. I walked through the garage, pulling out my door keys, but found the back door was still unlocked. Walking into the kitchen, the sight of the sandwich, untouched on the counter where I had left it, stopped me cold.

I am not an anxious man by nature, nor do I worry unnecessarily. At that moment I knew something was wrong. Seriously wrong. I felt as though a cold, powerful, invisible hand had reached down inside my stomach and begun to squeeze.

Immediately I became concerned for Doe, fearing she might have had another asthma attack. I thought maybe she had collapsed somewhere on the premises and was lying unconscious, unable to answer.

I searched the house thoroughly, calling out again and again for Doe. I looked in every closet, even under the beds. Ours is a modern house whose attic is too shallow to stand up in and it is separated into two sections. There are two different places for access with pull down steps in the ceiling. I went to each, pulling down the steps, climbing up and sticking my head into the hot, dark space, calling, "Doe! Doe! Where are you?"

I went outside in front and looked around. No Doe. I walked back to the barn. I looked under and in everything. Still no Doe.

Then I climbed into the golf cart and rode all over and around our property, looking for Doe and calling her name. This cart had been a surprise gift from me to Doe, and she had complained about my extravagance at first, yet soon enjoyed using it to ride around our 150 acres.

Behind the house the land falls away to a long pasture. This field of deep hay has a rough track through it, evidence of our many trips in the cart to our pond, a favorite spot of ours.

I drove past the pine trees, down the hill behind the house. I stopped several times in the hay field calling, "Doe! Doe! Doe!" No answer. I went down to a site where we bury trash and looked there. She wasn't there. I followed the track to the end of the field, turned right and climbed again to a long line of trees. Through an opening in the trees, the track winds part way up a hill to an enormous oak. The tree rises from a tangle of thick roots, its limbs stretched out over the small pond where Doe and I loved to come and feed the fish.

I parked under the large oak tree, got out and walked all around water's edge, shouting, "Doe! Doe?" I stood in the late afternoon sun, sweat pouring off my face, calling, listening, but hearing nothing. That powerful hand inside my guts began tightening its grip again.

I rode the cart back to the house and went into the kitchen. It was unlike Doe to go off without leaving a note, but I still hoped that maybe she was with one of her women friends who might have dropped by unexpectedly.

I called Brenda Williamson. In my concern, I wasted no time in pleasantries. The first words out of my mouth were, "Brenda, where's my wife?"

Brenda Williamson

I remember that conversation well. Too well. I responded, "Allen, I haven't seen her today. She hasn't been by."

He said, "Well, the house door's open—been open since noon."

Knowing Doe, I said, "She'll show up, Allen. She must be out back or somewhere close by."

He persisted, "I looked around, with the cart, too."

"I'm sorry, Allen, but I can't talk now. Both my refrigerators are out and the man's here to fix them. It's crazy. My sister's crying over my nephew's condition and I'm supposed to be over at Mama's by 6:00. I just can't talk now."

"Do you think…?"

"She'll show up in a minute. Quit worrying. It's not like she's been *kidnapped* or anything. I just can't talk now, ok?"

Those words haunt me still.

Allen

After Brenda hung up, I decided to call Doe's other close friends from church, Malinda Lancaster and Charles Lord's wife, Sylvia. My hands shook as I pulled out our church directory. I turned quickly past the two pages of the color pictures to the address listings in the back. The calls were useless. Like Brenda, neither Malinda nor Sylvia had seen or heard from Doe that day.

I became alarmed then, and started calling the family. I called Brenda Keith; my nephew, Bill Simmons; my sister Jean; and Doe's nephew, William Paul Knox. I told them all Doe was missing.

These calls took several minutes. Brenda Keith arrived

immediately, and was coming in the back door when the phone rang. I picked up the receiver, praying it was Doe, while Brenda stood on the other side of the kitchen counter. With the first words I heard, that chilly hand inside my gut reached out and squeezed again.

The caller spoke with an oriental accent, his English broken, in a high-pitched, almost falsetto voice, and difficult to understand, "Your wife with me. Unharmed. If you don't do what we say, we bust her head in. We want $100,000. I want you go in and take tape out of answering machine and bring outside and crush in drive. I want you not call police on this."

Did you ever watch a movie and think, "Well, if that happened to me I would...?" You don't know what you will do until it happens to you. You don't get to practice. All you get is one shot. I've laid awake and replayed that conversation in my mind a thousand times, thinking if only I had said this or demanded that, but I promised to do everything he said. I didn't argue with him a bit. Only later did I realize that the caller did not tell me where to take the money or how we would make the exchange for Doe.

I could barely tell Brenda what he had said because I was shaking so hard. But I did get another tape and crushed it with my heel out in the middle of the driveway in case someone was watching. I later turned over the actual message tape to the F.B.I. Since I had not recorded the ransom call, there was nothing else on it pertaining to the kidnapper.

I called Bill Simmons at the auto parts store, sometime after 5:00. Bill and Doe were close. Bill, my older sister's son, had grown up working with us in the store. When Doe and I retired, we left the auto parts business in his hands. Bill, unlike me, is a large man, has real physical strength, and is as close to me as any son could be. He has a good mind and I trust him completely. When he came to the phone, I just blurted out, "They've taken her!"

"What?"

I told him, "Somebody has taken your Aunt Doe."

"Wait, slow down, Uncle Allen. Tell me what's going on."

I described the ransom call, including the instructions to destroy the tape, and Bill asked, "Did you do that, Uncle Allen?"

"Yes, I did."

"Well, I'll be there in just a few minutes. You have to call the police, Uncle Allen."

"He told me not to call the police."

"We have to, Uncle Allen."

After I hung up the phone, Brenda Keith and I talked about what we should do. We realized that we did not have any control over the situation. I figured I would need more help and had to turn to the police. Once we decided to call them, we were afraid to use my phone in case the kidnapper had some way of monitoring our calls.

I called up to the Williamsons' and their daughter Sondra answered the phone. Sondra was sick and had stayed home from work. She said that, after the refrigerator repairman left, Brenda drove to her mother's house in Memphis. I told Sondra I needed to use their phone without telling her anything else. Bill waited for me to call him back, and we then made plans to meet at the Williamson's house. I next called my sister Jean and Doe's nephew, William Paul Knox, again, to tell him.

William Paul, in addition to being a home builder, has a paint contracting business as well as a retail paint store. I knew he kept large amounts of money on hand. On a Friday night, he would be my quickest source for ready cash. The kidnapper had not mentioned where or how to give him the money he was demanding. I assumed this was a scare tactic.

It was working. I thought he would call back anytime and I wanted to have the cash together when he called. After filling him in on what had happened, I asked, "William Paul, can you get your hands on some cash?"

"I don't know, Uncle Allen, how much are you talking about?"

I told him, "I need seventy to eighty thousand dollars. Surely you can raise that."

"I'll get what I can. How much time have I got?"

"I don't know. We haven't been called back."

"I'll start gathering the cash and come to you."

I drove the short distance to the Williamsons, parked in the drive, and went in through the carport. Entering this way, I walked through Brenda's craft room, totally unaware at the time of the silk flowers and ribbons spilling over everywhere. I climbed the steps into the kitchen and greeted Sondra bluntly with, "Where's your phone book?"

The Williamson's kitchen is a small area divided in half by free-hanging cabinets over a counter. On one side is the breakfast table, and on the other are the sink, stove and refrigerator. The phone is on the wall by the door into the den. Sondra handed me the phone book. Balancing it on the butcher block table, I fumbled through the blue pages for Federal Government listing and found the number for the FBI. It was well after 5 o'clock, but someone answered the phone. I told them about Doe and the ransom call, but they told me that at this time it would be a police matter.

I already said Eads is too small to have a police department. Our community falls under the jurisdiction of the Shelby County Sheriff. The only man I knew then at the sheriff's department was someone I had known since he was a child, Rudy Davis, the son of our old friends, Henry and Bea Davis. I called and asked for Rudy. He wasn't there. They let me talk to somebody else and I said, "My wife, Doe

Roberts, is missing. Someone just called and made a ransom demand."

During these calls Sondra was standing right there with me in her mother's kitchen, hearing that Doe had been taken. After I called the sheriff, I went outside their house to wait for the deputies to arrive. Sondra called her grandmother's house to tell her mother to come straight back home.

There was a good hour of daylight left, maybe more, when I started waiting. I'd been outside most of the day, so the late afternoon heat didn't bother me. When Brenda arrived Sondra came out and told her what was going on. She couldn't believe it. She brought us some lawn chairs to sit in. Brenda was fanning herself with a newspaper. She gave me a part of it so I could also stir the air, but instead I used it to swat at mosquitoes, which were starting up their nightly search for dinner and I didn't want to be the target.

Brenda said for me to come inside into the air conditioned coolness, but I could do only one thing—wait. And I was already in the best place to wait, sitting and watching the street, to see the first glimpse of them. I was looking for a black-and-white car, by instinct I guess. But, of course, detectives drive unmarked sedans. It took a long time for them to arrive. My supporters who were there tell me that it was about an hour.

The light was fading, but it was still a beautiful clear summer day. I could hear the birds chirping and singing. Doe and I knew the calls of all our local species, and had learned to pinpoint within about a week the times when migratory birds came visiting. I was so numb I was glad the mosquitoes kept nipping me. My hands and feet moved in habitual patterns; I was not conscious of my body's needs—no hunger or thirst, no knowledge of an uncomfortable shoe, nothing. Except, at the same time, I noticed myself trembling. And that persistent fist inside my stomach would not let go. It kept squeezing, tighter and tighter. I didn't think then I was in shock, or even a mild form of it, but I guess I was. I could not have stood up for long.

A little over two hours had passed since that voice said he had Doe. How could he have Doe? He would be restraining her in some way. Doe in pain. A shudder ran through me. I shut my eyes and thought, *I am not in pain, I am looking around and everything is quiet and normal, but Doe is in pain. We should be hurrying. Let's hurry. Doe needs us now, but we are not hurrying. The minutes are barely passing, and while I am sitting here, Doe is somewhere nearby.* I felt a scream starting, then opened my eyes, looked around, and tried to reassure myself that everything was normal there in Brenda's yard.

And what else was happening to Doe? A man had her, I talked to him and he had a foreign accent. What was he doing to Doe? I could not imagine. My brain was on fire. Here the yard was so quiet and peaceful, and I was just sitting in that chair, an ordinary yard chair, a little bent, frayed plastic strips holding it together and supporting my weight.

I watched for the police car and for Doe, too. I thought, *why am I looking for Doe? She's not going to walk up here. She's not going to be in the squad car. Why am I looking over there by the driveway for her to walk up? I can see her now, her face looking out the window from the back seat; how she will see me, get out of the car and run toward me. She will know I have been waiting for her, right here at Brenda's. They will have told her I am waiting. And I will rush to her, give her a big hug and a sweet, long kiss, and she will explain everything. It will be over in a few minutes. Doe will tell me what happened. If anybody can get out of a jam, Doe can.*

This all seemed a temporary madness. Why would anybody kidnap Doe? Well, if it was money they were after, I could raise it. We had plenty of money, that's how most conflicts get resolved. Money. That would fix everything.

Doe was not merely a good woman; she was the best I've ever known. Well, I haven't known many, but Martha Eudora Jones was head and shoulders above all others: ambitious, resourceful, highly intelligent, a mind of her own, but also a good listener.

Doe took me as I was, and wasn't a "nagger" as some husbands say. Instead, I say she was my "reminder-er." I counted on her to keep me straight about most things. She was good at taking care of day-to-day things, and she saw that I did my share. I didn't volunteer about household things like husbands need to do, but when she gave instructions, I took them. I wanted to. I didn't have to give her any. She was in charge and she'd be on top of this so-called kidnapping, too! Why, her kidnapper would start listening to Doe and know she was right, whatever the problem was.

This couldn't be a real kidnapping, not like the ones you see on TV. This was just a simple community, here, more of a crossroads than a town. There was nothing going on here, just folks doing normal things. Folks are not "normal," really. Not any of us. We all have our peculiarities. But around here no one I knew was controversial, perverted, weird, or wishing to be somewhere else. We folks in Eads chose to be here. We didn't consider ourselves humble, understanding that "humble" is a synonym for poor or simple, but we were simple in a lifestyle that included everybody I could think of in this small community.

Some of the ladies put on a few airs, and occasionally a man might want to make sure you knew he succeeded in business. But, we were all here in Eads because we wanted to be, and we wanted to live simple lives, staying at home, mostly.

Doe and I wanted to succeed. We wanted to find a way to have more material wealth than our parents, if we could. We would have done fine if we hadn't become wealthy. We did succeed financially, but we never lorded it over those who had less. We never made a practice of noticing or even caring what others made in their jobs. We'd lived peaceably and in harmony with our neighbors, having known most everybody around these parts for many years.

It felt unnatural, sitting there waiting for the police. In my entire life I'd rarely ever called the police, firemen, or even an ambulance—either for myself or even a neighbor. Hadn't needed to. But at that moment I felt totally helpless. I knew I needed all the help I could get.

In business, we gain experience in making decisions. Some have to be made without having all the necessary information we need, so we proceed on assumption and rely on advice from others whose judgment we trust. Bill Simmons and I worked together as a father and son would, maybe better. Knowing that he was on the way and would be arriving soon prevented me from breaking down. It kept the whirlwind in my head from taking over. Bill's strong arm would support us both.

Tears welled up in my eyes, but I held them back, blinking hard and looking for his car.

While I waited, the thought occurred that I should go look for Doe. I forgot for a split second that a kidnapper had called me. I was denying that something violent and evil had already happened. I now understand that happened in the minds of others as well. A neighbor confided in me, months later, that she held out hope that Doe had run away, that she had left me, that she was safe and would come back someday. No such luck.

When my long wait ended, it felt as though a circus had come. Probably ten to fifteen cars converged on the Williamsons' home. I didn't think it was necessary for me to tell law enforcement what to do, but they swarmed in like a bunch of locusts, with no subtlety whatsoever, and the whole neighborhood knew right away that something bad had happened.

CHAPTER TWO

Allen

There are few houses on George R. James Road. The only vehicles usually seen on the road belong to the people who live on it. The road makes a ninety-degree turn in front of our property. About a quarter- mile north, a dead end spur heads east off George R. James Road. This is where the Williamsons lived. A circular driveway in front is long enough for several vehicles; that night the police cars filled it up.

Brenda Williamson

My recollection of that night's events differs somewhat from Allen's. I believe the Shelby County officers made some effort to hide their presence as they arrived, to keep appearances normal on George R. James Road. We had discussions with them which centered on how to move back and forth between our property and Allen's without detection. To both Allen and me such efforts seem ludicrous now.

Allen

The news spread quickly to our family members, each calling another. William Paul called his parents. His mother, Doe's older sister Jewell, lives north of Memphis, out from Dyersburg. Jewel Knox has the same iron gray hair and dark brown eyes as her sister Doe.

Jewel Knox

I recall that Friday vividly, when I had set up my one-woman flea market on the side of the highway.

My husband Herbert came down and told me he thought I should pack up and come on home.

I protested, "It's not dark yet and I've already sold over a $100."

But he said, "Well, come on. Pack it up and come on. I got to tell you something important."

So I loaded up my old white van and drove to our home. It sits on the highway and is marked by an old trailer parked on one side. Herbert did not tell me anything until we were inside.

He closed the door and, without warning, said, "Doe's missing."

Shocked and surprised at what I heard, I asked him, "What do you mean?"

"Well, they think somebody's kidnapped her. William Paul called just a while ago."

I felt shock and horror upon hearing the news, asking myself, "Who on earth would do that to Doe?"

Allen

My older sister, Jean Simmons, who lives in Memphis, began calling our family with the news that Doe had been kidnapped. Many in the family didn't believe her at first.

Jean left several frantic messages for our younger sister, Wilhelmina, on her tape machine in Houston, Texas. Unknown to Jean, "Willy," as Wilhelmina is known in the family, was driving to Memphis to play golf and bridge with old friends. Willy missed her Memphis friends and had returned for such visits several times since moving to Texas. The fact that Willy didn't tell us about this visit later seemed suspicious to the FBI. She got into town around 9:30 p.m. that Friday and planned to spend the night with a friend. Half an hour later Willy's husband Ken called her with the news.

* * *

At the Williamsons' residence, Bill Simmons stood near me in the kitchen while Inspector Ramona Swain questioned me. Inspector Swain is a large, thickset brunette with a formidable personality and more than a match for any man in the field of law enforcement. After her initial questions, she decided to call in the FBI and requested they come out immediately.

The agents got lost trying to find the Williamsons' house. When they finally arrived, sometime after 9:00, the questioning began again in earnest. Brenda says my demeanor that night seemed detached, emotionless, almost cold. Yet the only thing cold I could remember was— inside my gut—that cold strong hand which kept squeezing away, until my stomach felt like it would burst.

The Knox brothers, Larry and William Paul, arrived sometime around 10:00. William Paul told me he had brought $60,000 with him and should have the rest the next morning. During Ramona Swain's questioning, Brenda Williamson remembered seeing a White Winnebago, a vehicle she did not recognize as belonging to anyone she knew, turn around in her drive earlier that day. After hearing about the Winnebago, William Paul seized on this possibility and decided to search for it himself. Bill Simmons decided he, too, would join the hunt.

Bill is an excellent shot with any firearm and, at that time, drove a metallic gray Porsche. He and the Knoxes are men of action. William Paul had worked as a repo man and felt like he could handle anything he encountered. At the time, William Paul carried at least one handgun on his person and kept quite an assortment in his truck.

Bill took off in one direction and the Knoxes in another, looking for the white Winnebago.

For Doe's and my sake, William Paul and Larry Knox headed off down Interstate 40, toward Memphis, checking vehicles at every exit and rest stop, then returned on the back roads, looking in vain for what might be Doe's kidnapper.

Willy telephoned to say she wanted to come out to the house, but Jean told her that the FBI would not allow visitors. Later my nephew, Bill, admitted to his mother and aunt that he was concerned for their safety and it was he, not the FBI, who did not want them to come out. Bill also wanted to keep things calm around me and thought my sisters would be anything but calm. Willy's friend drove her to Brenda Williamson's instead. They were at the Williamson's for two or three hours. I also called my brother that late afternoon and James came over immediately.

Brenda Williamson

I consider myself as a person who wears her heart on her sleeve. It is hard for me to control my emotions and I definitely lost it that night. When Inspector Ramona Swain came in, at first I felt comfortable with her, but was surprised by Ramona's immediately antagonistic attitude towards Allen.

Having known Doe and Allen so well, I couldn't believe how suspicious the investigators were.

Allen

I was so numb that I did not pick up on Ramona's antagonism toward me. All I could think was, if only I had begun looking for Doe at noon, what would have happened?

The hours stretched on without another call from the kidnapper. At various times, Brenda Keith and I swapped places so there was always someone at my house in case the kidnapper called back.

By midnight, after no further developments, everyone left Brenda's. She called her husband, a Memphis fireman, who was on duty that night and knew nothing about this. Brenda also asked permission to call our pastor at Eads Methodist, James DeBardeleban. She still bears hard feelings for the pastor's response to the situation. When Brenda told Brother Jim that Doe had been kidnapped, his response was a perfunctory, "Thanks for calling," and then hung up.

At our house, the FBI agents had arranged for the phone company to install recording equipment and a "trap" to capture numbers and locations of incoming calls. The FBI set up all their equipment in the kitchen. Our kitchen is a long rectangle with an "L" shaped counter at one end where the wall phone is located. Opposite this counter is a reverse "L" formed by the sink, stove and more cabinets. At the far end is the breakfast table by a large picture window. I sat at the table with some of the agents while others settled down in the den on the couch by the fireplace.

William Paul Knox and Leonard Jones, Doe's brother, continued searching from Lakeland to Collierville until sometime after 1:00 a.m. They called to see if there was any news, and I told them we had heard that Shelby County officers found a white Winnebago at a motel, but it was only tourists who had taken the wrong exit and gotten lost. That whole incident had been a false alarm.

William Paul told me he called his mother close to midnight and said, "Now, Mama, don't you worry. We've got the roads all blocked and we'll find Aunt Doe before daylight."

At the house, I sat with the agents and deputies talking until around 2:30 a.m. Finally there was nothing more to say, and I went to bed. I left the agents around the breakfast table, where they talked in low tones through the rest of the night. I learned that, from time to time, they would take a turn walking the grounds, moving cautiously.

Outside the house everything seemed normal. The night was quiet, but country quiet, full of the sounds of crickets and tree frogs. The temperature, so cool on Wednesday, had returned to August-normal by 2:00 a.m.—humidity and temperature both in the mid-80's.

I prayed for some insight, some answer. I prayed that I would dream about Doe and she would talk to me, guide me, perhaps tell where she was being held. Then I slept as soundly as anybody ever could sleep. I have felt guilty about it ever since. How could I have slept at all without Doe beside me?

CHAPTER THREE

Saturday, August 8

William Paul Knox went to bed about 3 a.m. He roused himself at 6:00 and went to open his paint store. After he picked up Lynn, his fiancée, he resumed his search. They were still looking for Winnebagos or anything out of the ordinary—anything that wasn't right. They drove across the river to West Memphis, Arkansas, and then back east as far as Jackson, Tennessee.

Allen

I woke that morning at my usual time, somewhere between 6:00 and 7:00 a.m. You know, when you first wake up, your mind has to play catch-up. I smelled coffee, and when I saw Doe wasn't there in the bed with me, I first thought she must have already gotten up. The next moment the truth hit me. Sick at heart. I rolled over. My clothes were still on the floor beside the bed where I dropped them the night before—silent evidence of Doe's absence. I stepped over them and retrieved a fresh pair of pants and shirt from the closet. I fumbled putting my belt on. I was trying to hurry and slow down at the same time. I could hear the rumble of conversation through the bedroom door.

When I walked into the kitchen, where several agents were sitting around our small breakfast table, they moved and gave me space to sit down. Brenda Keith was there and poured me a cup of coffee. Later I tried to eat, but that powerful cold hand on my stomach wouldn't let me keep anything down. No sooner than I finished some eggs and toast, I felt them rising within me and rushed to the bathroom, where they came back up.

* * *

My younger sister Willy hadn't gotten any sleep and called Jean early that Saturday morning.

My older sister Jean told Willy the FBI was still restricting visitors. Willy accepted this for about thirty minutes and then decided, the hell with it, she was going!

She called Jean back and told her she was on her way in spite of any FBI restrictions and Jean said she would meet her here.

Both sisters could tell I was in terrible shape. I wept openly several times that day. I was already regretting the call that had brought in the FBI. I felt I had lost all negotiating room with the kidnapper and given up any chance of getting Doe back alive.

You have to understand what Doe meant to my family. Willy was a child when Doe and I started dating. Willy always said she thought Doe was so pretty. As a schoolgirl and pre-teenager, Willy would ride the bus to downtown Memphis and go to the picture show. Then she would visit Roger's Café where Doe was working as a waitress. Doe would always bring Willy a hamburger and a coke. Such things mean a lot to girls. She used to take Willy shopping too, just the two of them. Willy often said she thought Doe was the best thing that had ever happened to our family. Our parents thought of Doe as a daughter immediately. The rest of the Roberts family made up their minds about Doe long before I did!

For as long as we were together, Doe acted as the peacemaker in our family. Any time a quarrel might start among the brothers or sisters in the Roberts family, Doe would come in like a volunteer fire brigade of one and stop it. She always knew how to appeal to reason in putting out simmering emotions.

Jean and Willy simply could not comprehend now how someone could have done this to Doe.

I had a .38 pistol in my dresser drawer and I holstered it in my belt. I wore it everyday, everywhere I went for two months. Bullets were in it, safety on, and extra cartridges in my pocket. I put change in the other pocket. If I was in a hurry, I thought my *instinct* would be to go to my left-hand pocket and that's where the bullets should be. No one asked me if I had a license and I didn't say I did not.

A license, technically a gun permit, in Shelby County costs three to four hundred dollars and you have to pass a firearm's proficiency test. A few classes were required and I went to them. Found out where they were, when they were, and attended. This gave me some purpose, actually, and I put stock in my ability to be doing something to help Doe. . . and protect myself. In my mind, I would constantly ready myself to have to draw the weapon. I *practiced* mentally and then I took to *practicing in reality.*

I did it, became proficient with a pistol, giving myself step-by-step directions, "Release the holster snap first, finger the safety as you draw, eyes this way or that." I practiced drawing both fast and slow, left and right positions. My inspiration, better described as a delusion, was the belief that my own skill might save Doe, or even myself, in a life-or-death situation.

A day was scheduled for me to go to the firing range and be checked out, but I didn't go. Why? I *can't* say. I just didn't go. I kept on carrying the pistol, and the FBI knew it, until mid-October.

I was anxious about getting the money ready for the caller. With the help of the FBI we made arrangements to meet both my stock broker and banker Saturday morning.

The drive to downtown Memphis took about 45 minutes. The National Bank of Commerce building is a combination of a 1920's Greek revival architecture on the east side joined to a modernistic, impressive high-rise office building on the west. It takes up a city block and fronts on the Mid-America Mall. From a vehicle, the south entrance to this fine structure is less than impressive: through a back alleyway and a narrow side door. On a Saturday morning no traffic interrupted us from Eads, and an Interstate connection put us right off on Riverside Drive. Bill negotiated an unexpected one-way street and there we were.

Doe and I may have come to downtown Memphis twice a year, no more. Recording deeds, or other real estate documents, brought me to the county courthouse occasionally; we kept meaning to see a Broadway traveling show at the renovated vaudeville theater, The Orpheum, a gorgeous, historic old building that seated about 3,000. That was another dream the kidnapper destroyed.

I felt a little better getting out of the house and going with Bill, even for this mission, raising ransom money. He stopped to get me a snack at a drive-through; I needed nourishment and was light-headed. Someone had eaten the sandwich I bought for Doe, on Friday, the day before, but not me. Eating a little now helped.

Yesterday at this time someone was pulling into my driveway, inducing Doc to open the door to our home. Or was she in the garden? I feel like she was in the house. She had dressed for the day; her yard sandals were still at home. When I left she had them on.

We believe Doe changed to black flats, a split-skirt—her favorite—and matching cotton top. Brenda Williamson went through Doe's closet and knew by elimination what Doe had picked out for Friday. She and Brenda did clothes shopping together; they both really loved a good bargain, sometimes even bought the same thing.

I was glad to be with Bill that Saturday morning. An officer asked to come along, but we refused. Bill and I both carried a sidearm, he may have had something more in the trunk, but I didn't ask. I believe we were followed, but so what, that was the least of my concerns.

Bill needed no assistance from the police. He was fiercely independent and had gotten along perfectly well without any help from them. For several years he had carried our store receipts to the bank on a daily basis. On those occasions he had a fast car and a gun in order to make our deposit on time and in safety.

He was the man for the job. His gray Porsche was a souped-up, powerful car with every luxury you could imagine. Bill's sheer body size and long legs somehow fit into his custom seat. He is about twice my size.

We took time to park in the pay garage for security reasons rather than the free alley and went in through the side door. A guard, on duty anyway I suppose, was looking for us. I had never been in the vault so had no idea what to expect. Doe had handled this for me and now I had to fend for myself.

We followed silently. I had an account with J. C. Bradford; their office was in the same building. I picked up a cashier's check from them for $100,000 and we headed for the Bank. We rode up the wrong elevator first, had to come back down to the lobby and start again. Bill broke into a sweat from exasperation; I was numb.

My teeth chattered in the cold air-conditioning. The lobby area is dim anyway, little daylight can reach the place, but it felt really dark that day. The bank lobby itself shares the entire first floor with the towers of elevators serving twenty-nine floors of office clients. Our footsteps on the black granite floor echoed above us as we crossed the deserted main lobby. An electronic chain partition gate separates the bank lobby from the office building lobby. The guard pressed a control button, the gate raised up, and we ducked under. Coming toward us was a man in a dark suit walking with authority. I had met him before and knew he was a senior bank officer, but he would not have known me at a social gathering, nor I him. He expressed concern, I think, but there was little conversation between us. Bill directed me and I followed his bidding, passing my check to the banker, who produced the money needed for ransom.

The bank lobby spread out around us, the tall ceilings and the massive marble columns made it feel so empty to me. There were sections of desks, camouflaged by potted foliage.

Doe never went in for fancy offices; she would see them only as an expense item, and could see the list of bills she would have to make out to pay for such. She had learned to stretch a dollar and never forgot the lesson.

Even here in the lobby of this bank, I felt Doe's presence. I had to keep reminding myself that it was Bill, not Doe, accompanying me. I would turn my head to speak to Doe and be surprised to see Bill. Doe would have liked to be there and see us stacking up all these bills from our bank account. Here was a carton full of twenties. She'd be proud we had it on hand to stack up and put in this ordinary box. She should be proud—she'd earned it.

We were here to get the money, a hundred thousand dollars, to exchange for Doe. $100,000. What a pittance. Doe and I had kept that much cash in a safety deposit box once so we could dip out of it whenever we wanted to, no questions asked even between the two of us. It was ours—we used it.

The kidnapper could have asked for everything I had and I would have given it to him. I had no feelings at all about the cash. It would have fit right in our briefcase, but Bill picked it up in the carton for me and we left.

A person in exchange for cash. I was not taking it in. The big, empty bank and the silence, that's what I remember about that Saturday morning. We exited the garage and paid the attendant. Our parking cost $1.00. Less than twenty minutes and we were on our way.

Bill, ever vigilant on the drive home, said little. As we pulled into the driveway, I felt more positive about our situation than I had since this whole experience had started. I was ready. Doe would be back soon.

CHAPTER FOUR

Allen

When we came into the kitchen there were about six or eight FBI agents in our little breakfast nook. Each one of them had me go over again and—in as much detail as I could muster—my account of what happened that Friday, minute by minute. A number of the agents gave me their home numbers, which I carefully recorded in my appointment book.

I do not remember the first time I met Agent Overall, who became the lead investigator for the FBI on this case, but she was among the group at my house that first weekend. Jo Anne is around 5'5", slender, fair-haired and always addressed me as "Mr. Roberts." Jo Anne's questions to Jean on Saturday were fairly general: Who was she? What were her children's names? Did she know of anyone who had anything against me or had tried to borrow money from me?

As we waited at the house for the next call from the kidnapper, the news of Doe's kidnapping continued to spread. The FBI hoped to keep the story from the media. In such circumstances, though, friends and family couldn't help but share their fears.

Karen Johnson

I was working at the post office that Saturday morning. A friend called me at home on Friday night with the word that something was seriously wrong at the Roberts home. She was not sure that evening as to what was wrong. I next received a call from a neighbor who told me that Doe was not just missing, but that she had been kidnapped. I stopped by Brenda Williamson's that afternoon on the way home from work, but Brenda wouldn't say much to me.

Malinda Lancaster

I got a call Saturday morning from a friend. When she asked me if I had heard that Doe had been kidnapped, I nearly lost my uppers. I thought she must be crazy. I couldn't believe it. I asked her how she had heard. She told me that the pastor of her Presbyterian church called and asked her to pray for Doe Roberts, who was missing. I called Brenda Williamson but she was so upset she told me she couldn't tell me anything more.

Brenda Williamson

The authorities told us to keep from saying anything to anybody. I really tried hard to follow their advice. I did not call anybody about Doe, and had been guarded in my remarks when others began to call me. I never expected that the most mundane chore would set me off on a crying jag over Doe.

My husband and I went to Kroger's to get some food to take to Allen and Doe's house. While I was at the grocery, I saw someone I knew and I just broke down. That was the first person I had told that Doe was missing, except for Sylvia Lord, who had called me and indicated she knew already that Doe hadn't been found. She said Allen had called her on Friday looking for Doe.

Then we went on to Allen's. That was the only time I went to the house because the detectives had pretty well secured it off.

Viola, my wife's older sister who was in her seventies at the time, told me she didn't hear the news until Saturday morning. She was driving to Mississippi from Rutherford, Tennessee, when her daughter's husband overtook her on the road and said, "Viola, you don't need to go to Mississippi. Sue doesn't want you to go. Turn around and let's go back to the house."

Viola said he wouldn't tell her anything until they got home. Jewell and Viola spent the rest of Saturday together, hoping to hear the news that their sister had been found.

During Saturday afternoon, the FBI advised me they had assumed formal jurisdiction. The Bureau does so whenever the presumption arises that the victim has been transported across state lines. Since Shelby County's southern border is Mississippi and the western border is Arkansas, the Bureau normally assumes formal jurisdiction twenty-four hours after a person disappears. With no further calls from the kidnapper, the agents were already asking questions among themselves about this occurrence. The typical kidnapper focuses on the money. Why hadn't he called back with instructions for the money?

The Bureau set up a command post in a motel on I-40 at Lakeland. In contrast to the quiet on George R. James Road, there was an intense level of activity there. They were really going to work on me, gathering information, building a dossier. It was obvious they were asking themselves, "Who is Allen Roberts and is he a likely suspect for the kidnapper?"

CHAPTER FIVE

Sunday, August 9ᵗʰ

Allen

Jean made breakfast Sunday morning. With it began a pattern which continued for months. I broke down and wept while I was trying to eat. I forced myself to eat the bacon, scrambled eggs and toast she had fixed. Then I got sick and lost whatever I had managed to swallow. Between meals I would regain my composure for a little while and then something else would trigger another crying jag.

Robert P. Wright had quite recently been appointed head of the Memphis FBI office. Wright had asked Agent Ed Bradberry to drive him out to the house. Ed called me and said they were coming. I told him to park the vehicle down by the barn and come in the back by the sliding glass door.

Tensions increased as the day progressed, while we all waited and the kidnapper did not call.

Once, when the phone rang, everyone took their position so the call would be recorded. I answered in the kitchen, looking towards the picture window. At the caller's first words, I knew it wasn't the kidnapper but a parishioner calling to express sympathy.

As I have already said, one hobby I shared with Doe was bird watching. One bird that is rarely sighted in our area is the red-billed woodpecker. Just after I answered the phone, I saw a red-billed woodpecker through the kitchen window. Excitedly, I pointed out the window, laid the receiver down, and exclaimed, "There he is!"

The officers reached for their weapons, and, right away there were at least eight pistols drawn and pointed towards the window. They must have thought I was moving away from the window out of fear, but I was only stepping around the counter to retrieve my Audubon Bird book! You don't know how you're going to react under such stress. Though Doe and I were avid bird watchers, I would have never guessed I would have reacted that way at that particular moment. I made the notation in the book—as I had a thousand times before, about one bird or another—about that particular woodpecker, as though nobody else was present, as the agents holstered their weapons.

My younger sister Willy admits to having a short fuse that first weekend. It was set off by her initial encounter with the FBI.

Sometime Sunday afternoon Jo Anne and Ramona Swain took her into one of the bedrooms and started grilling her. She grew angry at a particular series of questions about her children's birthdays. They tried to mix her up about the dates.

This went on and on, until finally she let fly, "You are not going to get me mixed up about my own children! What does any of this have to do about Doe? Why aren't you people doing anything?" Then she stormed out of the room.

Jean, our older sister, concentrated on taking care of me. Willy would get into arguments with the agents because she felt they weren't doing anything. When she was introduced to Agent Wright when he arrived, she could contain herself no longer and let him have it. She was so angry she appeared close to hysteria.

Bill Simmons intervened and said, "Come on, Aunt Willy, we'll go look for Aunt Doe." He then escorted her outside, where they got into Doe's cart, and "calling up the dogs," set out to search the property for themselves.

During those first few days after Doe's disappearance,

Bill Simmons remained physically close by me, yet he was never questioned by the agents handling the case. Even now he doesn't understand why this was so. He is the man nearest to me, like a son, and the most knowledgeable about my business and personal affairs. Yet the agents never took him aside, not that weekend nor any time in the months to come.

By late Sunday evening there was still no further word from the kidnapper. I wept frequently. I would regain my composure only to have some other trigger set me off again.

I didn't go to church that first Sunday. I simply couldn't. I was an emotional wreck. Later they told me how tense the small groups were in the recreation hall before church.

Ronald Cline

The story had spread with the warning throughout the congregation of Eads United Methodist Church: "Don't talk, don't tell."

Strangely enough, I do not remember Rev. DeBardeleban saying anything about Doe's disappearance during the service.

Brenda Williamson

Everyone in church that morning was afraid they might say something they shouldn't. I remember some of the members hurrying away immediately after the service.

Others, including me, drew together. Charles Lord spoke to our group about how quiet Doe had seemed at the meeting on Wednesday evening. That was a keen observation, but what did he mean by it?

CHAPTER SIX

Second week of August, 1992

Allen

By Monday, word of the kidnapping had reached the media. The reporters were besieging the house with calls. Although Agent Bradberry, the media coordinator for the Bureau, advised me not to make the kidnapping public, I decided to make a media announcement, hoping to force the kidnapper to call back. Bradberry called the local television stations, and they set up the press conference for Tuesday at the Eads Civic Club. I worked on my statement whenever I could compose myself, drafting and revising it.

During this time, the absence of further instructions from the kidnapper forced the FBI to consider alternative explanations as to Doe's disappearance. Unknown to me, Agent Jo Anne Overall began taking a hard look at me and my family. They became suspicious of Brenda Keith immediately. She was my only alibi for Friday and the only witness to the ransom call.

Brenda Williamson

Despite Doe's having been kidnapped, I had decided to go ahead with the opening of my shop at the Jackson Mall. The kiosk there is a small alcove where sprays of silk flowers cascade down the walls. There are no partitions to hide private conversation, so when Agent Overall and Inspector Swain came by on Monday, their presence was obvious to everyone passing. They stayed and questioned me, between customers, for hours that first day.

Their suspicions of Allen were evident from the start. They probed for whatever knowledge I had about Allen and Doe's relationship. For the first time that day I heard from them a statistic which would be repeated many times, "Over 95% of the murder/kidnapping cases involve family members."

Allen

On Tuesday morning, August 11, Bill Simmons and his brother Allen drove me to the Civic Center for the press conference. Ed Bradberry rode with us. When we arrived at the center, I was so distraught I had trouble getting out of the car and had to be helped. Ed had made it clear to all the reporters that I would not answer any questions. Under the white glare of TV lights and camera flashes, I gave my statement, asking the kidnapper to contact me, pleading for mercy because of Doe's asthma.

I stood there where we had danced so many times. The lights, cameras, the shouted questions, the press of reporters seemed so alien to our Civic Center. When I finished, and despite Bradberry's admonitions, the questions erupted as Bill helped me out of the hall and back to the car.

Ed Bradberry

When I left Allen Roberts after his press conference and returned to the Bureau's offices in Memphis, I met with Agent Overall and our superior Bob Wright. I told them I didn't think anyone could fake such physical and emotional distress and that I sincerely believed Mr. Roberts had nothing to do with his wife's kidnapping.

Allen

Tuesday and Wednesday passed without further calls from the kidnapper. The longer the time passed without him calling, the less sympathetic to me the law enforcement officers, with the exception of Ed Bradberry, seemed. I didn't leave the house. I talked with Brenda Keith on a regular basis and turned over to her the daily direction of the building business.

Against the advice of the FBI, I offered a $10,000 reward for information that would lead us to Doe. The agents feared that they would be flooded with crank calls. I made a statement to the press Thursday, August 13th, but no one came forward with any new information. Each day seemed endless. I tried to keep busy, but found it difficult to concentrate long on any task.

I had no idea then, but the FBI was busy checking up on me. While Jo Anne talked with Brenda Williamson, other agents questioned the Johnsons.

Carl, who is a building contractor, has a stocky, compact build, reddish hair, and strong, square features that look right at home on the little league ball field where he coaches his son's team. Karen Johnson is an attractive brunette. She was a real civic leader in our community until she had to devote more time to her children. The Johnsons, unlike other church members, were never intimidated by the FBI.

Carl Johnson

We will never forget the first time the agents came to our home. When the two agents came to our house, the first thing that happened was one asked to use the phone and the other asked to use the bathroom. Karen and I remember looking at each other and wondering if the agents were planting bugs. We really thought that our phone might have been tapped. For sometime afterwards, I would start phone conversations,

"Now, if anyone is listening…."

When the agents came back to our living room and started to question us, I challenged them on their lack of activity during the first couple of days after Doe's disappearance. I felt strongly that their failure to question the neighbors immediately cost the investigation precious information that was forgotten several days later. When the agents asked us about Allen and Doe, I told them that day, and kept telling them, that there was no way Allen could have harmed Doe.

This first visit was fairly short, no more than fifteen minutes.

Agents also came out to the building sites on Orr Road, checking up on Allen's activities during the Friday Doe was taken. I had been doing some work on one of Allen's houses, but I didn't see him that Friday. One of our workers said that someone had come looking for Allen and Brenda that morning and another one of the crew had seen them laying the sod at the house on Orr Road.

Karen Johnson

I wanted so badly to visit Allen, but was hesitant to go by myself because of the presence of the FBI. So, I called the Williamsons' and asked Brenda to go with me. Brenda agreed.

I picked Brenda up and we drove on down to Allen's. The FBI let us in and we visited for a short while.

I felt extremely close to Doe. Allen and Doe had set up a trust fund for our sons. Doe had been a witness just a couple weeks before at the christening of our new baby girl. After the service, Doe told me they wanted to do something for the little girl like they had done for the boys.

My father Ron Cline once told me that Allen once

commented to him what a rich man Ron was. Somewhat taken aback, my father had protested, but Allen explained that Ron's wealth was in his children and grandchildren.

For all their wealth and material success, the Roberts had not been blessed with any offspring. My father, Carl and I, all deeply appreciated the kindnesses the Roberts had shown our children.

Ann Richmond

The news of Doe's kidnapping didn't reach Gus and me until Tuesday. We had belonged to Eads Methodist for over forty years. I was close to retirement as a Mathematics Advisor for the Memphis Board of Education. My career had spanned the turbulence and stress of the Sixties and Seventies. Our church had been my support during the tense years when the Memphis City Schools were being integrated. Gus and I had been to a family reunion and did not hear of Doe's disappearance until our return late Tuesday, after Allen's statement was aired on television.

No one from the church had called us, I think, because of the "Don't Talk!" warning.

Our In-service Training for the new school year started that week. I was at a school meeting when a teacher came up and said, "Tell me about it!"

Puzzled, I responded, "Tell you about what?"

"Doe Roberts—don't you know about the kidnapping?"

That's how I found out. I think Gus had already heard when I got home that evening. I called Miriam Foley to find out what was going on. Miriam is a tall blonde with blue eyes. Tim is a man of medium build with graying hair. Both are sensible people and not prone to gossip. A friend or neighbor could always turn to them to learn the truth about a local situation in the Eads community.

Miriam Foley

Tim and I had been in Nashville visiting my daughter. Our next door neighbors, Lloyd and Doris Hight, were also church members. As soon as we drove into our driveway, Doris telephoned to say she had something to tell us in person. I remember her coming straight over, sitting down in our living room and saying, "Doe Roberts has been kidnapped!"

I could not believe what Doris had just said. Those words left me flabbergasted and I started crying.

Doris went on, "They told us in church this morning that we are not to speak of it. It is not open to the press. We are not to tell anybody, because the newspapers and television would get hold of it. The FBI doesn't want that to happen for a while."

Allen

The Foleys and the Hights lived on Great Oaks Road, directly off Seward Road, which winds and twists some distance southeast of the church, just across the Fayette County line. The houses on Great Oaks all sit far back from the road on large lots of rolling hills dotted with trees and ponds. Lon and Malinda Lancaster lived across from Doris and Miriam. Charles and Sylvia Lord lived at the eastern end of Great Oaks, where the road stops abruptly at a line of trees.

These church members and neighbors would soon find themselves intertwined in the drama of Doe's disappearance and eventually pay a high price for their proximity to one another.

Mike and Mary Coward

The newest church members at the time of Doe's kidnapping were Mike and Mary Coward. They had built their dream home a few miles west of the church. Mike is tall, broad shouldered, and balding, with an open, honest face that matches his up-front, what-you-see-is-what-you-get, demeanor. Mary is a soft spoken, lovely woman who lets Mike do most of the talking. Mike has his own insurance agency and is an avid deer hunter. Mary gives most of her time to taking care of their young grandson. Like the rest of the congregation at Eads Methodist, they are intelligent and articulate people who have worked hard all their lives.

The Cowards had built their home on a large, almost five acre lot. They set the house far back from the road, hidden in a thickly wooded hillside. Mary loves the quiet and being surrounded by the trees, especially in the spring when the wild dogwoods lace the woods with white.

Once the Cowards moved into their new home, they felt strongly that, in order to become part of the community, they should go to the Methodist church closest to them. They immediately liked the congregation at Eads United Methodist.

The Sunday the Cowards joined the Eads United Methodist Church, Mary was home with a bad asthma attack, so Mike spoke for their whole family. After church, Charles Lord came to him and told him the church wanted him to be Chairman of the Church Board.

Mike was flattered, but not ready to jump aboard such a position of responsibility right after having become a member.

When Mary and he joined, they had just come from a large church heavily involved in fund raisers for a building program. Though they thought they would enjoy being members of this small church, they soon began to question why more wasn't being done in this area. When Mike asked

Charles Lord about doing some spaghetti suppers or other fund raising activities to increase Doe's Building Fund, he told Mike that such things weren't done at Eads Methodist— if they needed money, they just wrote a check.

Not letting himself be put off by Charles, Mike approached Allen Roberts with some of these ideas and Allen seemed much more receptive.

Allen

When Mike and I started the Breakfast Club, Charles' attitude again was most negative. Mike said he wasn't looking for any more jobs. He had his own insurance agency and had been heavily involved at their former church, but thought my idea about the Men's Club was a good one. The men needed something to do together for fellowship like the women.

The first time I saw Mike after Doe disappeared, he asked me to come over sometime for dinner. I immediately asked when.

"What about today?"

I told him, "That'll be fine. I'll be there in a little bit."

Mike and Mary Coward

Allen had dinner with the Cowards that night. They saw him at church off and on the next few weeks, but anytime he came, his tears and theirs started as soon as he came through the back door.

This whole thing got to the Cowards. Mike is a large man who always thought that anything he could get his hands on—kick or hit—he could handle. Their involvement in this was different from anything he had ever encountered. There was nobody and no thing he could place his hands on. . . . It was with him all day, all night. He went to bed with it at night, and the next morning it was still there, unsolved.

The whole Doe matter loomed over the Cowards and stayed with them. They felt there wasn't anybody at the church who wasn't greatly affected by this. It was obvious when they attended church the Sunday after Doe's kidnapping.

They started talking about Doe that Sunday and have never stopped.

The congregation decided to have a prayer vigil on August 16th for Doe. The Cowards didn't go. Mike thinks he had an appointment that night anyway, but Mary was having a hard time with it all.

The Prayer Vigil

When it came time for the service to start, the church was surrounded by vehicles from local television stations. The church members were outnumbered by the media. That first night no one knew quite how to handle this intrusion. Camera crews filmed as the congregation prayed for Doe's return.

Ann Richmond

When we decided to have this first vigil, Brother Jim said he couldn't do it; he was so upset he just couldn't deal with it. So our former pastor, Brother Nance, came and led the service.

We all have our weaknesses. Brother Jim has his strong points—he gives the sweetest funeral service of anybody I've ever heard. He has a way of pulling things together to make it personal. He gives good sermons, he teaches rather than preaches. His sermons are not about hellfire and damnation, but about God's love.

Brother Jim did not know any better than the rest of us how to handle the media. At that first vigil service Charles Lord was our spokesman. He gave a moving talk about what a wonderful person Doe was.

Before they were stopped, the media even filmed our congregation praying at the communion rail. Some of the members were outraged at this intrusion and told Brother Jim that we didn't want them filming during our services anymore. So many Sundays the film crews and reporters would be waiting in the parking lot when we came outside.

Allen

After standing watch for over a week, the FBI decamped. Willy went back to Texas for a few days. Jean stayed on. I worked at staying busy around the house and only left for short errands. I went to church on Sunday morning, August 16th, the anniversary of Elvis Presley's death.

Brenda Williamson

It wasn't until August 16th that I went back to church. Allen and his sister Jean were there. We sat together at our regular pew in the back and cried most of the time. Being there was just too hard for me. I didn't return for almost five years.

Mary Linda Rose

As church pianist, I went to Brother Jim that Sunday and said, "Let's open the doors of the church. Maybe something will happen."

Brother Jim's response was, "You set it up, Mary.

Whatever you want to do."

I was disappointed in Brother Jim's leadership in this crisis.

We did have several services. Because Brother Jim wasn't up to it, Brother Nance, our former pastor led one, and Charles Lord stepped up and acted as a lay pastor several times. He would say, "Let's keep praying and keep these doors open for Doe."

One service I prayed several hours. I thought we needed to have a time and place to go and cry and pray. We weren't going to Allen's house because we were told that was off limits. I wanted something to pull us together and I really thought, once we did, Doe would walk through the door.

Doe gave me a spiritual treasure, not once but several times. I work at the hospital and she made these wonderful little toys for us to give the children. When we would get ready to give children a shot, I would hand them one of these little puppets with a smiling face on one side and a frown on the other. I'd tell them that a lady named Miss Doe made it just for them.

Doe also collected unopened Kleenex boxes and other similar hygiene items to take out to the nursing home. We had a couple from the church that was in the nursing home. Doe visited them regularly. You always knew when Doe was getting ready for another visit because she would have all the items she had collected stacked up in her pew that Sunday morning.

Allen

After the FBI left my home, a terrible quiet descended. When Willy came back the last week of August, the story was old news, and the media was no longer showing any interest. Willy wanted to keep everyone aware that Doe was still out there, somewhere. She decided to put up yellow ribbons around the community.

Willy obtained yards of ribbon and florist wire from Brenda Williamson. My sisters stayed up all that night making hundreds of large bows from two-inch wide ribbon. They hung the bows on trees and fences up and down George R. James Road and Seward Road as far as the Civic Club.

I had some leaflets printed with Doe's picture and offering the reward, and put them up wherever we could. The national square dancers magazine gave over a full page to an article with a picture of Doe and me asking for information, but August ended without any further calls from the kidnapper and no news of Doe.

Like any brother and sister, Jean and I began to get on each other's nerves. As August passed into September, I finally told Jean she should go home. I worked at whatever of my business could be done from the house. I also worked in the garden and drove to the pond to feed the fish alone.

Alone. I realized, more than ever, I was alone. This was so hard. Doe and I had been true partners. Inseparable. We had worked together all our married lives. I had no idea how difficult it would be to live alone. We were gregarious people and had always sought the company of other folks in our activities. Now for the first time in my adult life, I went to sleep in an empty house and had to face that emptiness again in the morning. I wanted so much at least to dream about her, but such dreams didn't come for a long time. As bad as this was, the worst was yet to come.

October, 1992

Allen

On October 8th, at 9:14 p.m., the kidnapper called me the second time. I had prepared for this moment by previously connecting my own tape recorder to the telephone. As soon as I recognized that strange voice, I punched the "record" button. The device unexpectedly gave a tone which he must have heard because he said, "You go pay phone at Mason and Collierville-Arlington Road. I call you there in four minutes." He hung up and I rushed to my car.

I barely made it in time to catch the ringing phone. It was him calling. He said, "If you want wife back, you bring me $185,000.00. Must be all in unmarked $20.00 bills. Anything else, you never see her again."

I said, "I can't have the money before Tuesday. Monday is Columbus Day, a bank holiday."

After a pause, he said, "I call you Tuesday and tell you where to take money." Then he hung up.

Tuesday came and went with no further word from the kidnapper.

CHAPTER SEVEN

November, 1992

Allen

For almost three months I had hoped, prayed, and waited for some news of Doe. In my heart, I'm an optimist who believes that man is basically good. As a Christian, I also believed in God, and that He is both good and omnipotent. But if that was the case, why had Doe been taken from me?

The FBI agents had become constant companions. One morning Jo Anne Overall called on me. She really had nothing new to add, just that she was "checking on me to see how I was doing."

I said, "I'm getting along as best I can under the circumstances." In truth I was *lonelier* than ever. Wilhelmina had gone back to Texas and I was alone. At home, everywhere I turned, I could see Doe's image. Never had I missed her more.

Jo Anne had attempted on past visits to lift my spirits with whatever encouragement she could muster. This morning, however, her mood was solemn. Her face grew somber. "I probably shouldn't say this, Mr. Roberts, but. . . ." Her voice trembled.

"Say what?" I asked. "What shouldn't you say?"

With a look of compassionate concern, she told me, "There's probably only about a one percent chance at this time that Doe is still alive."

After she left, those words haunted me. In my heart and mind, I'd faced each day with the understanding that, as time passed, the odds grew greater and greater that Doe wouldn't be coming back. But to hear that assessment coming from someone else, especially someone in the profession of criminal investigation and law enforcement, drove the point home.

I've always tried to be realistic. The reality I had to face was that Doe wasn't coming back. Without her, what did I have?

Even though it was early November, the weather was sunny and pleasant, nothing like the feelings storming inside me. I put on my jacket and walked, in a daze, down to the orchard behind our home. Each step I took echoed the refrain, "Doe isn't coming back."

The dry leaves were beginning to turn. Soon they would fall to the ground and winter would be here for me to face alone. Could I? For forty-four years there had been one person with me through everything, good and bad, helping me build and hold our world together. She had been a part of me and I had been a part of her. I realized I had no identity apart from Doe. How could I go on?

I reached the far end of the orchard and turned to walk back to the house. Again, with each footstep, I thought, "Doe isn't coming back. Doe isn't coming back!" I saw her face in front of me, her dark eyes shining with love for me. I thought of how much I loved her, how much I missed her, how painfully aware I was of her absence. *How painfully aware I was of being alone.*

When I reached the gate leading from the orchard, I looked toward the sky, where God was supposed to be. "Do I really want to go on living?" I asked. For that one moment I considered ending it all. What did I have to live for without Doe? I might as well kill myself right then.

Every night of my adult life I have prayed. I never made it a practice to ask God for specific things, except after Doe disappeared, when I asked Him if she might reveal something to me in my dreams. But my sleep had been deep and dreamless. It had seemed God hadn't, or didn't, want to listen to my prayers.

At the orchard gate, however, it came to me in a blinding flash. I *wasn't ready* to leave this life. Dead or alive, Doe had to be found, that was my first purpose. And even if Doe wasn't coming back, she would never have wanted me to give up. As much as she loved me, she would want me to find other important reasons to go on living, and to have purpose and meaning in my life. Where would I find those things?

Again the answer came. Where had Doe and I found the most happiness together?

Square dancing.

Maybe my church had failed me, with most of its members turning their hearts, if not their faces from me. But that wasn't so with the Top Spinners. They were waiting for me to return to them. Suddenly I was ready to go.

CHAPTER EIGHT

The Perpetrator

I've done a *very bad thing!* After living an exemplary life, why would I do this?

Nobody must find out. Nobody!

Right now nobody else knows—*and nobody ever will!*

As bad as what I've done is, there's still a very good chance I'll get away with it.

I was so careful! Nobody knew except Doe. She won't be telling anybody. Right, Doe? It's our little secret.

As for you, Allen. . . .Why did you have to be so smug and secure in your success? We all know you have money. The way you spent it, or *wouldn't*, was enough to drive anybody crazy. All those capital improvements to the Eads United Methodist Church, so you'd look like the Great Benefactor.

Then there was the Eads Civic Center you helped found and build so you and Doe would have a nearby place you could go do your stupid square dancing.

But when I came to you with an investment. . . .Well, you didn't exactly laugh in my face, Allen, but you made it clear you didn't think much about it. You obviously don't think much of me, either. Everyone else does. They come into my fine home and see the wall in my den with the awards, plaques, citations, and certificates. They look up to me for my long and distinguished career of service and respect me for my financial expertise. That last is a joke!

But it's on me. Me and my bad investments and borrowing to support a false lifestyle. It all had to catch up sooner or later.

Now it has. But maybe, just maybe, you'll come through with that ransom money, Allen. If you do I still have to collect it without getting caught.

I'm betting I can do it.

CHAPTER NINE

Esther Hammons

After twenty seven years of independent living as a widow, the last thing I ever expected was to get involved in a serious relationship with a man again. But when I first saw Allen Roberts after Doe's disappearance, when he returned to the Top Spinners Club again in November of 1992, my heart ached for that poor man. These were feelings of compassion, almost pity, certainly not for a romantic attachment.

He seemed so nice, yet so lonely and so lost! He and Doe had been key members of the club. Both were quite good square dancers. I had only been coming to the club for a few months. I had seen the Roberts and knew who they were. Like everyone else, I was caught up in the events, fearing for Doe's welfare and hoping for her safe return. Some tongues were already wagging, as soon as he came back dancing, that he had no business returning without Doe.

Having lived through the suicide of my husband, I was no stranger to the depth of feelings men are not supposed to have or show. I knew what those feelings could drive a man to do in a fit of self-destruction. I guess that, when I saw Allen then, I realized how vulnerable he was. He didn't know me from Adam's house cat, so what could I do? I would dance with him in my turn, along with the other lady members, but he and I really never had any serious conversations.

Then something happened to change all that. At our meeting, which was right before Thanksgiving, several members were discussing their plans for the holiday. Allen was among that group, listening politely as the others spoke.

Even though he was physically present, I could sense his mind was elsewhere, probably fixed on Doe. On an impulse, I said, "Allen, I am having dinner at my daughter Pat's home and you are welcome to join us."

Almost as soon as I finished speaking, I worried that others might take what I said as being too forward. How would Allen respond? I held my breath and waited for him to speak. He blinked, then cleared his throat. In a soft voice that I could still hear, he told me, "Thank you, but I'm having dinner then at my niece Sheila's house."

At our December meeting, Allen approached me and started talking about square dancing. As he spoke, I noticed he was studying my name badge. Nothing happened that night, but, the next day, he telephoned me.

"Would you like to have dinner with me tonight?" he asked.

"I wish I could," I replied. "I am taking my granddaughter Ashley to Bellevue Baptist Church tonight to see the Singing Christmas Tree Show." I had been going for the past 15 years and looked forward to it. Maybe Allen would like it, too. On an impulse, I asked, "Would you like to come with us?"

He did not hesitate a moment. "Yes."

The three of us attended the program and enjoyed it very much, except Ashley, all of twelve years old, was coming down with a fever. She felt ill and we took her back to her parents' as soon as the show was over. Then Allen came home with me, where I fixed us some cold cuts and crackers. Although the television set was on, we spent the time talking about everything and nothing. Always, always, Doe must have been in the back of both of our minds. I found myself enjoying the company of this gentle, caring man perhaps too much. Especially knowing he was technically still married. He was such a good listener, and seemed so interested in everything I had to say. He stayed until midnight, when I simply had to tell him goodnight because I had to work the next day in my own salon, keeping the full schedule of appointments I had with my loyal clients.

At my front door, instead of the "Methodist handshake" I expected, Allen Roberts took me into his arms and kissed me. It was warm and tender, not merely a thank-you or a brotherly kiss. To my complete surprise, I found myself kissing him back!

When we broke apart, I saw tears well up in his eyes and trickle down his cheeks.

"I'll call you tomorrow," he said. Then he was gone.

Oh, Lord, where was this headed? I wondered if I would hear from him again, the next day or ever.

CHAPTER TEN

Esther

The next morning at my shop I received a phone call from Allen. "Hon," he asked, "can you come to dinner with me tonight?"

I hadn't thought he would contact me again this soon. I knew my evening was clear. "Where did you have in mind?"

"Red Lobster. The one near you in Raleigh."

This popular chain of seafood restaurants had good food and a reasonably priced menu with a pleasant atmosphere. I had been there before and liked it. I responded, "M-m-m, that sounds like fun. Can you come about six?"

"I'll see you then."

Allen arrived at my front door dressed in a gray suit, white dress shirt, and red tie—more formal than I expected. Still, I wore one of my best dresses and was prepared for the evening.

At Red Lobster we both ordered the seafood platter. Allen sipped on a soft drink and I had iced tea. We settled into a routine of small talk, the get-to-know-each-other kind. Stuff like, "How was your day?"

Right after our orders arrived, Allen burst into tears. These weren't the quiet, dignified tears I'd seen him shed as he said goodbye to me the night before. Instead it was more like a dam had burst inside him. He was trying bravely to hold back, but I could tell he was losing the fight.

He busied himself holding his eyeglasses in one hand and the other dabbing his face with a white handkerchief. Placing his glasses on the table, he shut his eyes and sobbed, "I'm sorry."

Without thinking, I reached across the table and squeezed his hand. "It's all right," I said. "You've been through so much."

Slowly he regained his composure and we finished our meal.

After we left the restaurant and were seated inside his car, the Volkswagen Doe had driven, Allen started crying again. I waited for him to get back in control, then said, "Allen, maybe it's not such a good idea for us to be seeing each other."

He turned and looked straight into my eyes. "It's not your fault, Hon. I'm glad that I can be with you—talk with you. You have no idea how *alone* I've been—how I've felt since Doe was taken from me. I need to be with someone besides my family. Do you follow me?"

"Yes. I think so."

That was when it dawned on me why I was with him. It had nothing to do with romance. Instead it was concern and the idea that, somehow, I might make a difference in the life of someone else. When I was a young wife I hadn't been able to see the warning signs of my husband's depression and resulting suicide. Now I was with another good man who was hurting and I wanted to help him. He needed me, and I would be there for him.

CHAPTER ELEVEN

From *The Commercial Appeal*, November 12, 1992:

ROBERTS HIKES REWARD TO $25,000
FOR SAFE RETURN OF MISSING WIFE

Source: Chris Conley

Businessman Allen C. Roberts, whose wife disappeared more than three months ago, Wednesday increased a reward for her safe return to $25,000. Roberts also said he received a second ransom call last month from a man with a foreign accent who demanded a large ransom in $20 bills in exchange for the businessman's wife, Martha "Doe" Roberts. The caller did not tell Allen Roberts where to take the money.

Doe Roberts, 65, was last seen by her husband the morning of Aug. 7 as he left the couple's 150-acre farm in Eads. She has since been the subject of an intense FBI investigation. The FBI has followed hundreds of leads without avail, FBI special agent Ed Bradberry said.

"It certainly is a puzzling case," he said. "But we do have leads, and it remains a top priority."

The FBI has interviewed employees, friends and business associates, conducted physical searches of the Roberts property and surrounding areas, and checked into several unidentified women found dead in other states. Bradberry said he is considering redoing parts of the investigation.

He has said Allen Roberts is not a suspect.

While Roberts has not given up, he said, "The thread I am clinging to is getting a lot thinner.

"Statistically, the odds are not in my wife's favor by a long shot," he said. "I'm frustrated; the kidnappers haven't followed through in a logical manner."

Roberts points to a second ransom call he received in early October. The call came from a pay telephone several miles from his home, but the caller did not say where to leave the money, Roberts said. The FBI refused to comment on the call.

A similar thing happened the day Doe Roberts disappeared, Allen Roberts said. He said he received the initial ransom call at 5:30 p.m. Aug. 7 from a man who threatened to kill his wife and demanded a $100,000 ransom. This caller did not say where to drop the money either, he said.

Allen Roberts believes he was drawn out of the house on Aug. 7 by a man who said he wanted to meet him at a house at a Fayette County subdivision Roberts is building. The man did not show up, and when Roberts returned home about 11:30 a.m., his wife's car was in the carport but she was not at home. The doors to the house were unlocked. Her asthma medicine was left behind.

When he returned about 4 p.m., she was still gone.

"The FBI investigated everything, but nothing led to anything," Roberts said.

Roberts said he has started square dancing again, an activity he and his wife enjoyed, "simply because I need to be with people. . . .It keeps my mind occupied."

He said he plans to leave the area after the beginning of the new year. "It wouldn't serve any purpose to stay here and be under this pressure," he said.

From *The Commercial Appeal*, November 21, 1992:

FBI RETURNS TO EADS HOME FOR CLUES

Source: Quentin Robinson

The FBI on Friday sent investigators to the home of a missing Shelby County woman to re-examine the property for evidence that might explain her disappearance. Doe Roberts, 65, was last seen by her husband the morning of August 7 as he left the couple's 150-acre farm in Eads. She has since been the subject of an intense FBI investigation. The FBI has followed hundreds of leads without avail, said FBI special agent Ed Bradberry.

He said agents returned to the farm Friday to search the property once more. Bradberry said agents are digging on the ground and searching throughout the property. They also are re-interviewing people, he said.

The new search was ordered because the investigation had come to a standstill and the FBI wanted to make sure they didn't overlook any evidence during earlier searches, Bradberry said.

Bradberry said the FBI still does not have a suspect in the woman's disappearance.

Businessman Allen C. Roberts, her husband, said he received a second ransom call last month from a man with a foreign accent who demanded a large ransom in $20 bills in exchange for her safe return.

Last week, Roberts increased a reward for her safe return to $25,000.

From *The Commercial Appeal*, November 24, 1992:

ROBERTS PLEADS FOR WORD FROM WIFE'S KIDNAPPERS

Source: Rob Johnson, with contribution by Staff Reporter James Kingsley.

Allen C. Roberts, the Eads man who says his wife was abducted nearly four months ago, pleaded Monday for her kidnappers to let him know that Martha Doe Roberts is still alive. He says he has stripped his phone of wiretaps and is just waiting for it to ring.

"All defensive measures have been removed," he said while standing in his blustery backyard Monday. "I want to make it easy for them."

After he is assured she is still alive he says, he promises to do anything the kidnappers demand in order to get her back.

The FBI has been investigating the bizarre case since Aug. 7. Since then, Roberts says he has received two calls from a man with a foreign accent demanding a ransom in small bills. The caller, Roberts said Monday, never has told him where to deliver the $185,000.

The FBI has interviewed employees, friends and business associates, searched the Roberts property and surrounding areas, and checked into the identities of several women found dead in other states.

Agents have said Roberts is not a suspect, but last week, they returned to Roberts' 150-acre spread in Eads with a backhoe to check out a spot Roberts has used as a dump.

Special Agent Ed Bradberry declined to comment on whether they found anything suspicious or informative.

''They're going back to Square One and reworking me,'' Roberts said Monday.

He also said that the agents on the case have been sensitive, even supportive, during the past four months, and he attributed last week's excavation to FBI supervisors, not to the field-level agents.

Roberts believes he was drawn out of the house on Aug. 7 by a man who said he wanted to meet him at a house at a Fayette County subdivision Roberts is building.

The man did not show up, and when Roberts returned home about 11:30 a.m., his 65-year-old wife's car was in the carport but she was not at home.

The doors to the house were unlocked. Her asthma medicine was left in the home.

Roberts has offered a $25,000 reward for her safe return.

Allen

We had done everything that could be done and still no word from the kidnapper. What we didn't understand was that he was changing his tactics: he'd spread his net beyond me to my neighbors.

Friends and Neighbors

Brenda Williamson and the Cowards began getting "hang-ups." When they answered the phone, there would be a moment of silence. Then the caller would hang up. At first they did not associate this harassment with Doe's disappearance.

Brenda Williamson

The caller terrorized me. He would only call her when my husband Will was on duty at the fire station. My daughter had recently moved out into her own apartment. That meant when Will was on duty in Memphis, I was alone at the house. I became so frightened that I began sleeping with a gun under my pillow.

When I drove around Eads, I would find myself looking for Doe's body along the roadside. When I returned home, I would dread the next ring of the phone.

When a call came, it would always begin the same—that high-pitched voice in an oriental accent, saying, "You Roberts woman's friend. Why you do nothing help her? Why her husband do nothing?" From there he would rant and rave about Doe not being well, needing medicine, and him needing money.

Friends and Neighbors

The kidnapper, using the same false voice and oriental accent he had used with Allen, began calling several other people and demanding that they make Allen pay the ransom. These calls began just after Thanksgiving Day. Brenda Keith, Ronald Cline, and Malinda Lancaster were each called during the first week in December. They found these calls both frightening and frustrating. Frightening because these average people were being telephoned by a real life criminal who had abducted a person they dearly loved. Frustrating because the caller's accent made him both annoying to hear and almost impossible to understand.

Malinda and her husband lived out on Great Oaks Road across from Miriam and Tim Foley, and from Doris and Lloyd Hight, just a few houses down from Charles and Sylvia Lord. She was the next to hear from the kidnapper.

Malinda Lancaster

I had not been regular in my attendance at Eads Methodist for some time. For the last couple of years I had been nursing my sick mother and had not returned after she died. I had still regularly attended the monthly meetings of the Homemakers Extension Club, another organization, unrelated to the Church, to which Doe and I both belonged.

The last time I saw Doe was on Tuesday before the Friday she was abducted.

I had driven that day, picking up Doe. We spent several hours together in Memphis at the luncheon meeting. I had been the president and Doe the treasurer of the no longer extant Eads Extension Homemakers Club. The two of us kept the group going, but had little success in getting others to help with the programs. After several years, Doe suggested that we disband and join the larger club in Memphis, which we did.

Since my husband's retirement he and I had talked about moving to Florida. At our age, we thought our house and yard had become too big for us. We loved Florida and that was where our son lived. I remember telling Doe about our plans to move, the week before Doe disappeared. Doe was upset by this news.

Doe's disappearance, then those awful telephone calls, made our last year of living on Great Oaks Road a nightmare.

The first call came on a Wednesday evening, early in December, around 8:35 p.m. My husband and I had settled down to watch a basketball game on television. I was sitting there in my gown, just as relaxed as could be, when the phone rang.

A high-pitched male voice said, "Doe Roberts asked me call you. You are her good friend. Her husband—he said to do this. Husband chance to. . . I talk Brenda Keith last night.

Her family don't care. Ask me three questions. I prove she here."

"Can I talk to her?"

"No! Ask three questions! Only three!"

"Well, what organization are we in together?"

There was a brief pause before he answered, "Extension Homemakers."

"How old am I?"

Again the pause. "66, 67."

"What church do I belong to?"

"Eads United Methodist Church. She say you not been in two–three years, but she go.

"Husband pay me to do this. You not prove this. Husband talk to Brenda Keith last night. Husband has girlfriend. Husband not honorable man. Have pictures of husband dancing with girlfriend. Husband not honorable. Do not call husband on telephone. He say telephone not bugged, but is. He call FBI last night. Know she is alive. Do not contact police. Good you not use telephone right away."

"What do you want me to do?"

"You go to husband. Tell him to contact me by 6:00 p.m. tomorrow or she not be alive. Blood on your hands. She cry. Beg me call you. Family not care. Husband don't care. I tired this. Want to depart this area."

That call almost sent me into a nervous breakdown. I have known Allen and Doe for years. I just didn't know who or what to believe—or what to do. My husband said, "Call the FBI." So that is what I did.

I called the number in the phone book and the person that answered said someone would call me back. FBI agents came out and put a recorder on my phone. There were three people at my house around the clock for almost a week.

They wouldn't let me talk to anyone or see anyone. My neighbor Miriam Foley came over to see what was going on and they wouldn't let her in. We have a couple of couches in the den. Two of the agents slept there.

While the agents were there, they received calls from other agents who were following Allen. He had started dating—going square dancing. This just blew our minds. This was not taken well by Doe's best friends.

The news reporters heard about the call I had received from the kidnapper and wanted me to make a statement, so the FBI wrote a statement for me, then drove me to the Civic Center to give it. They told me to say this and nothing more.

I read, "My name is Malinda Lancaster. I am a close personal friend of Doe Roberts. I have been her closest friend for many years. My purpose in calling this press conference is to communicate with the person or persons who know where my dear friend Doe is. Timing of the press conference is based on the fact that I was in contact with a man last night who convinced me through a series of questions that only Doe would know that Doe was still alive.

"I know what is going on here. I'm having this conference because I believe that the people holding Doe want to deal with me rather a member of Doe's family and I want them to know I will do everything necessary to insure Doe's safety. I have the necessary money to meet the demands required for Doe's safe return. It is important for these people to somehow communicate with me again so that I might provide the money that is required and that they provide me with necessary instructions so the transfer can be made. I beg the person holding Doe to release her safely. I will comply with whatever arrangements are necessary."

The caller did not call back while the FBI was there. He did not call back for some time. When he did, he wouldn't let me say anything. He would just give his little spiel,

"Roberts man not honorable. Make him pay me. You make him pay." Then he would hang up.

I recorded that call, then phoned Agent Jo Anne Overall and told her I had the tape. She told me not to touch it, but I accidentally erased it when I thought I was rewinding it.

After I had gotten about four calls, our son who is a Memphis policeman became concerned. He's been on the force since 1973 and is on the Tact Unit. He came out and took us to the firing range. He gave us his old service revolver and taught us how to shoot with it. He wanted us to keep it with us in case something happened. You know, we just didn't know what was going on or where this might lead.

I talked with Brenda Williamson from time to time. I felt so sorry for her. She was getting all those same sinister calls and the caller would hang up. Brenda didn't know what was happening. She was such a sweet person and she was so frightened.

After Doe disappeared, I heard that Allen had started going out with other women. While the FBI agents were at my house, I heard them on the phone talking about following him and who he was with. It was so hard not to believe that he wasn't involved. Doe was my friend and I just couldn't turn her away.

The FBI told me not to contact Allen, not to have anything to do with him. Then later they said that they thought it was strange Allen never made any attempt to contact me after I got all those calls. That seemed suspicious to Jo Anne and Ramona.

Jo Anne is a slender woman, about 5'4" and she is sort of a nervous type. She got a lot thinner during this investigation. They didn't tell us anything, ever. We had to tell them and share everything with them, but not the other way around, and we didn't like that.

* * *

74

From *The Commercial Appeal*, December 4, 1992:

FRIEND OF DOE ROBERTS SAYS
CAPTOR CALLED HER

*Source: Rob Johnson, with contribution
by Staff Reporter James Kingsley.*

A woman claiming to be Doe Roberts's best friend says she heard from the captors of the missing Eads woman Wednesday night and is convinced she's still alive. During a hurriedly called press conference at the Eads Civic Center Thursday, Malinda Lancaster delivered a typed statement, reading to Roberts's captors from an underlined passage: "I know what is going on here." She promised to deliver ransom for Roberts's release, but would not take questions after reading the statement.

Martha 'Doe' Roberts, 65, was last seen Aug. 7 by her husband, retired businessman Allen C. Roberts, at their 150-acre spread in east Shelby County. She has since been the subject of an intense FBI investigation that has sent agents out to chase hundreds of leads.

Her husband has claimed to have received two telephone calls from a man with a foreign accent claiming to be his wife's captor, but he says the man has never told him where to deliver the $185,000 ransom.

Roberts, reached by telephone at his home Thursday night, said Lancaster had not contacted him about receiving new ransom demands, but added that he believes what she said is true.

"I want to give her all the leeway in the world," said Roberts, who added that he heard about Lancaster's press conference from the media. "If she can come about and bring about the return of my wife, she will have my undying gratitude."

Roberts has offered a $25,000 reward for the safe return of his wife. "I have been a failure," he said. "They (abductors) haven't followed up on me at all. I must have done something wrong. I wish it could work out."

The FBI has said Roberts is not a suspect, but last month they returned to his rural property with a backhoe to unearth a small dump in a search for evidence. The FBI has not said whether anything was found.

Thursday's late-afternoon press conference was the latest strange turn in the bizarre case.

Lancaster crossed the rear lawn of the cabin-like community center and handed out typed statements, uneasily asking each reporter and cameraman assembled whether they were members of the press.

"The timing of the press conference is based on the fact that I was in contact with a man last night who convinced me through a series of questions that only Doe would know that Doe is still alive," she said.

Furthermore, she said, "I am having this conference because I believe the people holding Doe wish to deal with me rather than a member of Doe's family, and I want them to know that I will do everything necessary to ensure Doe's safe return."

FBI spokesman Ed Bradberry would not say whether the agency was aware of Lancaster's remarks.

He said the FBI had nothing new to say about the kidnapping.

Ronald Cline

My first call came soon after Brenda Keith and Malinda

Lancaster had gotten theirs. I could barely understand what the caller was saying. I asked, "You mean Doe is still alive?"

"Yes, I talk Roberts woman this week."

In other calls, the caller threatened to split Doe's head open, but that night he said if I didn't do what he said, he would cut her arm off.

After the call I was shaking so hard I could barely talk. I called Allen first. He told me to call the FBI. That's what I did every time I got a call. I phoned him first to let him know. He always told me to call the FBI. Some who got calls didn't phone Allen, but I always called him.

When I talked to the FBI agent, I think his name was Rick, he told me, "Now just settle down." He could tell that I was torn to pieces. You know, I went through World War II, but nothing upset me like these calls.

Allen

At Eads Methodist, there had been several prayer vigils for Doe. Some of the members felt that the pastor did not take the leadership role he should have in such a crisis. Charles Lord helped fill in the gap. One of the church women later told me she felt Charles became their spiritual leader during that time. It was Charles who led the prayer vigils and dealt with the media whenever they intruded on the services.

He and Sylvia had always been pillars of the church— real workers. That's always appreciated in a small congregation.

Some years before, our church membership had been quite a bit larger. The Methodist district changed pastors and about that time, people began leaving the church. By the time Doe was taken, the church was down to only about thirty families.

In November Charles Lord began telling people at church he had a friend in the Secret Service, and he was working closely with the FBI to find Doe. Charles also said he was concerned about Allen carrying a gun. He called me one afternoon and then came by my home. He said, "Some FBI people want to meet with us at the Shoney's on Sycamore View."

I didn't want to go. I felt like I shouldn't have. I didn't want to do something behind Allen's back. He had always been so good to me and my family.

Charles persisted, saying, "They want to talk to us. It's important and we should go."

I didn't understand why they wanted to talk to me. What did I know?

Finally after Charles kept on and on, I went down there with him. When we arrived we met two agents, one was a white lady and the other a black man. We got in their car, and the first thing I saw was a shotgun mounted on the ceiling. Charles and the agents kept bringing up about Allen carrying a gun. I don't remember the rest of the conversation. I finally realized what Charles and the FBI wanted me to do was talk Allen into not carrying a gun.

I looked up at that shotgun on the ceiling and I said, "Well, in my opinion, Mr. Allen ought to carry a gun, and in fact, he ought to have two. His wife has been taken, we don't know who did it and his life could be in danger, too." I shut up after that.

On the way home, I told Charles, "If I were in Allen's place, I would carry a gun."

The next time I saw Charles was at the Church, where he suggested we raise some "snitch money." He thought his friend in the Secret Service could find out something about Doe.

Allen

Charles Lord called me one afternoon in mid November and asked me if I would help repair a door at the church. When I got there, Charles was in his truck and motioned for me to get in.

As soon as I had sat in the truck Charles began, "The real reason I called you was to talk about Doe."

"Okay. Talk away."

"Well, in the first place, I want to assure you I'm not recording this conversation."

"Okay." I sounded like it didn't matter to me, but of course it did. Why would Charles even mention recording our words? We were supposed to be friends. That only made me suspicious and defensive.

Then he pulled out a tape recorder and showed me there was no tape in it. I couldn't help but think, *well, what about any other tape recorders you're hiding?* But I didn't say anything. I wasn't worried because I had nothing to hide.

"Let's get away from here," he said.

He drove us away from the Church, out towards Bartlett. His pitch to me was that he had a friend in the Secret Service who owed him a big favor. Charles said that this favor was so huge that this man would jeopardize his career, his pension, anything for Charles Lord.

He said, "This man is used to dealing with the criminal element. If you'll give me $25,000, I believe he could turn up Doe's kidnapper real pronto."

I said, "Well, Charles, I'll think about it."

Whenever I don't like a deal, rather than say "no," I say, "I'll think about it." That gives me a back door in case I change my mind. I heard later that Charles talked to several people at church about raising this snitch money, but nothing ever came of it. I had already offered a reward of $25,000 which had not brought any real help. If Charles' contact could deliver, why didn't he take me up on my reward offer?

By Christmas, my relationship with the folks at church was noticeably strained. Doe's women friends were really down on me about my resuming square dancing. There were several friends whom I asked to be my square dance partners, and I was asking friends to go out and eat with me. This was the behavior that got everyone so upset. I didn't know it at the time, but there were small things being said among our church friends— little things that weren't true, and some of them, really most of them—outright lies.

Those little lies seemed to grow very quickly into big ones. I assumed that people who had known me for years would know that I was innocent and stand behind me, but gossip was undermining my good name.

Stories started to spread that I had never paid any taxes, that I had been unfaithful to Doe, that I paid someone to kill her. I couldn't conceive that people would believe such things.

I remember one incident in particular that hurt me so much. Sylvia Lord called me about a church project she and Doe had been working on. When we finished chatting, she asked me if there was anything that she could do for me. I said, "Yes, there is, Sylvia. I don't want you to believe that I kidnapped Doe or had anything to do with her kidnapping."

In a strained voice, she responded, "I'll try."

That hurt me worse than anything. I remember it so well because I dwelled on those doubting words: "I'll try."

CHAPTER TWELVE

Allen

I went square dancing almost every night. Everywhere I went I talked about Doe and what had happened. I talked to anyone and everyone who would listen. One of the square dancers I met was Esther Hammons, a small, attractive brunette whom I quickly learned had been a widow for over twenty years. She surprised me, pleasantly, at the November meeting of Top Spinners, when she invited me to join her family and her for Thanksgiving dinner. I appreciated her kindness, but had to decline because I'd already made plans to be with my sister Jean and her family.

Then, the week after Malinda Lancaster's media announcement, Esther asked me and I agreed to take her and her young granddaughter to Bellevue Baptist Church's "Singing Christmas Tree" program. In short order Esther became my regular square dance partner and dinner partner. Some in my family were critical of our friendship, but I don't think I would have made it through that terrible year without her.

At Christmas, I went through Doe's things and found a number of handmade gifts she had made and labeled with the intention of giving them to her friends before she disappeared in August. One of these was for Hazel Richmond, a neighbor and a church member at Eads United Methodist.

Hazel Richmond

In 1992, Doe was my secret pal in the Methodist Women's group. We drew names at the beginning of each year. Pals are not revealed until Christmas when gifts are exchanged. Unknown to me it was Doe who had left the small surprise gifts, such as flowers on my porch throughout that year. The Christmas after Doe disappeared, Allen sent me a beautiful mauve afghan that Doe had completed and even wrapped before her disappearance in August.

My husband built our house in Eads not too far from the Roberts'. I had formed the habit of walking down George R. James Road. Often, when things had been tough at school, I would grab my tennis shoes and walk even before going into the house. I did not think it was fair to unload my work frustrations at home, so I walked them off. I had walked the morning of Doe's abduction, but saw nothing suspicious.

Later, Charles Lord was one of those at church who came down on Allen. I was walking one morning in September when Charles drove by in his pickup. He stopped, rolled his window down, and said, "Hazel, don't you know it's dangerous for you to walk so close to Allen Roberts' place?"

I told him, "Charles, I do not believe any such thing!" I just kept on walking.

I still find it difficult to talk about that year. I rarely participated in the activities of the neighbors over in the Wildwood neighborhood where a number of the church members lived. The years between 1988 and 1993 were a time of walking with death. Doe's disappearance came on the heels of a series of deaths among my family, including the sudden and unexpected death of my husband, Mike.

I'm a retired elementary school principal, and will not tolerate rumors and gossip. When other church members started conversation about Doe's case, I insisted that they stop. I never received any calls from the kidnapper and refused to listen when snide suggestions were made about Allen. I thought Allen and Doe were made for each other and never believed Allen could have killed her.

Some of our friends were visited again and again by the

FBI. I knew that they called on Brenda Williamson on numerous occasions, at times daily, to talk about neighbors and friends and anything that Doe might have said to her during their friendship. As time wore on and the investigation continued, it seemed the one of our church friends that Jo Anne used as a principal source for information was Charles Lord. As the retired controller at the Defense Depot he probably had some high level of security clearance and must have looked like a valuable resource to the investigators. Charles evidently was seeing the FBI on a weekly basis and hearing negative things about me.

The Meeting with Mike Coward and Charles Lord

By January Mike and Mary had begun to hear rumors about Allen running around with different women. The rumors continued, and, as a friend of Allen's, Mike admits hating hearing them because they tarnished the image of a man he dearly admired and respected. So, when Charles proposed that Mike and he get together and talk with Allen, man to man, Mike agreed.

Charles suggested, "Call Allen and ask him to come to your insurance office on church business. I'll happen to be there and we can confront him then."

When Allen came, he acted surprised to see Charles there. He and Charles got into a "sandpaper situation" immediately. Charles started by saying, "Allen, it's not helping your image for you to be running around with all these women, square dancing while Doe's still missing."

Allen countered, "I'm here to talk about the church. My own personal life is off limits." With that, Allen got up and walked out.

Afterwards Charles said that, if Mike told the FBI about the meeting, Lord would have them all over Mike's office like Lord had them at his own house all the time. Mike didn't want that.

Evidently Allen went home, and at some point told Jo Ann Overall about the get-together at Mike's office.

Jo Anne telephoned Mike and asked him about that meeting—who was there, why, etc.

He responded that they were concerned about Allen and thought they should talk to him.

When she asked whose idea it was, Mike answered that it was his. Why he said that, he now says he'll never understand.

Jo Anne asked him if he was sure, and he said he was. That was because Charles had asked him not to tell the FBI he had suggested the meeting. Looking back, Mike knew it did not make sense if Charles was supposed to be working so close with the FBI.

In the beginning, Mike and Mary felt there was no way they would believe that Allen could or would have hurt Doe. Then they heard all these rumors, and began to think that two plus two was going to equal four whether they liked it or not.

The Perpetrator

Well, it's good to know how I've got them all going. Miriam Foley called up Sylvia Lord suggesting they refinance their houses to raise the ransom, since it looked like Allen wouldn't spring for it. Even though Sylvia went ballistic over the thought, I'll take odds Miriam and others who love Doe so much will go for it. Then I'll get that money after all.

Ronald Cline

The calls resumed. In his latest, the caller said, "You find key to riddle in the street." It didn't make sense, but I guess that's what riddles are all about. I called Allen and told him, adding, "I'm so tired of sitting around and doing nothing, Allen."

He said, "Let's try this. You live only a couple of hundred yards from the church. The kidnapper seems to check on you regularly. Put a sign in your driveway saying, 'Meet me at Kroger.' On the date and time given, we'll be waiting."

Allen

In addition to Ronald and his son-in-law, my good friend Carl Johnson, I asked my nephew Bill Simmons, and Charles Lord to meet at Ronald's house that night. Ronald lives in a two-story, white frame house on Jefferson, just a few hundred yards from the church. The house sits close to the road. I thought that anyone driving by could see the sign on the car. . . and the kidnapper would, too.

My plan was for Bill to keep the money and go off in his own truck with a CB radio. I'd be in communication with him from my truck. He was to park somewhere near the Kroger on Highway 64, where he could keep us in view, but we would not know his location. I felt that it was too dangerous for the money to be with us; we might be robbed of it and still not have Doe. If the kidnapper made contact, and I was assured Doe was alive, then and only then would I call Bill to come in with the money.

Standing there in Ron's living room. I made it clear that I didn't want anyone risking their lives.

My speech was primarily for Bill Simmons' benefit. Of all those present, I was most worried about his doing something foolhardy. Doe and he were close. He had practically grown up in the Auto Parts Store. Before we stopped working at the store, if Doe had some problem and felt she couldn't discuss it with me, Bill was usually the first one she talked to. Like me, I knew he would have done anything to get her back.

Bill knew Carl and Ron, but had never met Charles Lord. I could tell he took an immediate dislike to Lord because of how Charles acted that night. As with members of the Church, Lord acted disdainful and arrogant toward Bill. I noticed Charles failed to offer Bill a handshake when they were introduced. That set Bill's opinion of Charles Lord forever.

We did not stay long, and soon I left with Bill in my truck. Ron Cline asked Charles to ride with him. Once inside, Bill informed me that, during a brief moment when I had left the room, Charles said in my absence, "If Allen doesn't think enough of Doe to do what has to be done to get her back, I will! I'm not afraid. I'll take the money to the kidnapper."

Bill told me he didn't say anything, but that he didn't like Lord's insinuations. He cautioned me to watch Charles Lord. I didn't think much of Bill's warning at the time because Charles acted that way with everybody.

Carl Johnson

Allen had not told the FBI about his plan—he emphasized that we were on our own. But when we pulled out on to Highway 64, a little red car with Arkansas tags followed us from Anderson's store. Charles looked back and said it looked like FBI agents were behind us. Then just as we got to the Kroger, the red car got in front and turned in ahead of us. We parked on the east side of the store near the pay phone. Allen parked his truck right next to us.

Someone had suggested—I forget who—that maybe one of us should go wait by the pay phone in case the kidnapper decided to call. Allen went and waited by the phone first.

The Kroger store is a new one, built in the last few years.

It has an entry/exit vestibule filled with shopping carts and vending machines. You enter on the right and exit on the left. The pay phone is by the exit door. While I was standing there, hoping the phone would ring, Mary Linda, Ann Richmond's daughter, came in with her own daughter. She naturally walked over to speak.

Mary Linda Rose

Melissa and I walked into Kroger and I said to her, "Well, there's Allen. Let's go over and speak to him."

We walked over gave him a hug. Then I asked, "What are you doing, Allen?"

He said, "Uh, I'm just waiting right here."

"What are you waiting on?"

"Well, I'm thinking the phone's gonna ring."

Allen was never a good liar. He didn't lie and never had to.

I said, "Have you been told there's going to be a phone call?"

"Yeah."

I said, "We'll wait with you."

I turned to Melissa and told her, "We've got time, don't we?"

We stood there a few moments and then Allen said, "Mary, you probably need to go on. This is not a good idea because you're standing here and they are out in the parking lot watching."

I asked, "Who's out in the parking lot watching?"

"Mary Linda, I'm watched wherever I go. I think I'm going to get a ransom call. I've got the money and you don't need to be here. I'm telling you this because I don't want you to be afraid of me."

Allen had said to me several times that he hoped that I was not afraid of him. I told him that night, as I had said before, "Allen, I am not afraid of you. You are our good friend. If it's okay with you, we'll stand here by you. I don't think you ought to be by yourself if the kidnapper calls."

We stood there and talked a while. Then the phone rang. Allen grabbed the receiver and sort of choked out, "Hello? Hello?"

The person on the other end didn't say anything. Allen finally hung up and we talked a little while longer. I saw his face had become flushed and he must have felt very frustrated.

Allen said, "I think we were seen together and that's why he won't talk to me."

I replied, "Well, I hope we haven't messed anything up, Allen."

"No, I'm just worried about you and Boo (Melissa's nickname)."

With that, we left.

Carl Johnson

When Allen came back from inside the Kroger store, Charles said he wanted to go next, but Allen pulled me aside and whispered, "I know Charles is a church member, and I really shouldn't feel this way, but I don't trust him. Will you or Ron go?"

Ron said he would, and went on inside the grocery building.

Bill Simmons and the FBI

Bill parked his car at the Mapco station across the street and waited in the cold. He couldn't make good visual contact and was about to leave when an FBI agent came to his car. They weren't supposed to know about Allen's plans and Bill asked him how they found out. The agent said Bill's group weren't very low key and had been easy to spot. Bill then moved on to the Amoco station and resumed his vigil.

All that happened for the rest of the night was that he got cold waiting.

Ronald Cline

We waited about two hours, but the kidnapper did not call. We went back home, cold and frustrated. The kidnapper called me the next Monday.

He said, "You did stupid thing Saturday night—have meeting and go Kroger store with FBI following you!"

Allen

My attempt to make something happen failed. That January was a cold, hard month in more ways than one. Things went down that I didn't know about. One was a second call from the kidnapper to Brenda Keith that she taped.

He had given her specific information about the amount of money he wanted, $190,000(up now another $5,000), and told Brenda exactly how many false drop points to give. Then, he directed her to have someone put the money down at the end of Great Oaks Road.

Brenda took down that information and called the FBI. They would not allow her to call me. Without my knowing it, the time for the drop came and passed.

When Jo Anne Overall finally told me about this, I confronted Brenda. "Why didn't you tell me?"

She grew defensive, saying, "Allen, you said you wouldn't pay the money unless you could talk to Doe."

"That's true, but you didn't even give me a chance to respond."

* * *

Over on Great Oaks Road, the caller was playing a lot of games with the church members who lived there. Charles Lord summoned several of the neighbors together for a meeting and told them he had received a number of calls from the kidnapper and had actually talked to a woman he was convinced was Doe. He said she had told him I would not pay the ransom.

At the end of this meeting, Sylvia Lord told several of the women she had also received a call one night. When the women inquired if Charles heard it, she told them yes, he was standing right next to her when the phone rang. She also indicated she was given the impression Doe was being sexually abused on a daily basis. Why the FBI never looked into this will always trouble me.

Miriam Foley

By late January I decided that the only way to get Doe back was for us to raise the money ourselves. I asked Charles to set up another meeting to work all this out. Charles agreed, but later that afternoon, Sylvia called it off and nothing came of all this

* * *

Allen

At the request of Jo Anne Overall, I took the lie detector test in January. I passed, but it didn't make any difference. Even though they heard about the results, the test didn't help my relationship with the folks at church. A story even went around that I had actually failed this test.

I think Jo Anne, deep down, believed in my innocence, but Ramona Swain was convinced I had killed my wife and was determined to prove it. The mysterious caller continued to confuse and terrorize everyone, which I believe was his objective.

Ronald Cline

I received several more calls from the kidnapper. We did manage to get a recording of one, but the FBI didn't even come out to hear it. Allen came over that night, picked up the tape and took it to them himself.

Carl Johnson

My first call came on February 4th. I was home alone about 9:00 that night. I didn't have any recording equipment, but did have a tiny note pad, about three inches long and no more than two inches wide. With the phone squeezed tightly between my ear and shoulder, I wrote furiously with a pencil as he talked,

He talked a long time, maybe five minutes or longer. He said, "I want $190,000 in twenty and fifty dollar bills, unmarked. Get four garbage bags. One to have the money in it. Others to have newspapers. Place one of the bags with newspapers in the Lancasters' driveway on Great Oaks; another at Macon and Chulahoma under the car parked in front of old store there. Place another bag with newspapers in your driveway and another on Bragg Road. I tell you later which one to have money in."

He said, "I give you twenty-four hours to make list of questions only Doe know answers. You get these from church members and square dancers and tell not to contact police."

I kept asking him, "Is Doe alive? I can get the money, that's no problem if she's alive."

"He kept saying 'You listen!' "

I told him, "No, you listen! I'm writing this down. If Doe's alive, we'll do anything you say, but we have to have proof she is alive."

He said, "If you get money together, she be released at Memphis airport or TV station. I see to that. Roberts, he not honorable, but I keep word."

He repeated this several times. I kept saying that Doe had to be alive; that this deal wouldn't work if she wasn't alive.

He also said he wasn't going to try to deal with Brenda Keith or Bill Simmons anymore because they didn't want to talk with him. I think Brenda told me that by this time she had started hanging up on him whenever he called. He also said something about Allen carrying a gun. He said he would call me the next evening at Anderton's restaurant in midtown Memphis around 7:30.

When he hung up, I called Allen first. He told me to call the FBI right away. Then Allen came to my home later that night and gave me several questions the answers to which only Doe would know. Allen also asked me if I would be willing to watch and see who came to get the money. I agreed. I knew all those places well and was sure I could hide at any of those locations and not be seen.

I was excited. I really thought we were going to get Doe back. I didn't go to work the next day. That night I went to Anderton's and waited all evening, but he never called. I didn't give up though. I thought surely he would call again.

When Allen and I talked about this, Allen asked me if I would be willing to take the money or go and watch over it. I told him sure. I was raised around here and know this area well. I felt I could position myself at any site and not be seen.

But that didn't happen. I didn't get another call.

Allen

The calls kept coming to everyone but me. By this time most of the folks at church had been telephoned. He called Charles and Sylvia Lord several times and one time left a bandanna in their mailbox that was supposed to belong to Doe. Jo Anne brought the red bandanna over to me to see if I recognized it.

She asked me, "Do you own a red bandanna?"

"Sure," I said, "several. I'll bring them out and show you."

I went and gathered all my bandannas. I had quite a few red ones. They were all different patterns. I told her they were all different because I bought them at different times, whenever I was out without a handkerchief and needed one. I told her I couldn't say whether the one she had was one of mine or not, though I thought I recognized it.

Friends and Neighbors

During this time Brenda Williamson was receiving hang-up calls while Will was on duty. This was before caller ID came about and it was very frustrating. There were several times when she thought someone might have been prowling around their property as well. She still wasn't sure that these calls had anything to do with the calls that the others were getting. One call made her certain though.

Brenda Williamson

One night in February after Doe's disappearance, the kidnapper called me when my husband was at home on vacation. Will told me to hang up and not worry about it, and I did as he said. Then, just minutes later, the FBI called me. They said that Charles had called them to report that the kidnapper had just called him after telephoning me.

Lord had told them the kidnapper said he had called me but wouldn't talk to me because I was alone.

The FBI asked if I was okay. I told them that I wasn't alone, that Will was with me. I tried to stay away from any involvement as much as possible because I felt everyone was trying to accuse Allen.

Allen

The third week in February "Unsolved Mysteries" aired a short segment about Doe's disappearance. The FBI said they received about twenty-five calls, but only five were handed on down to the Memphis office. The only thing the show did was make me more of a target. I began getting calls from women all over the country proposing marriage. Any other time I might have been flattered or amused, but when I thought that things could not be worse, the caller thrust us further into a deeper hell.

CHAPTER THIRTEEN

Allen

My friend Ronald Cline is blessed in his children and grandchildren. I am blessed with their friendship. Ron, his daughter Karen Johnson, and her husband Carl never once lost faith in my innocence. The kidnapper made them pay a terrible price for that friendship.

Ronald Cline

The first week in March, I was home alone around 9 o'clock that evening when the phone rang. As soon as I heard that voice, I grabbed the tape recorder, wrestling with it while trying to understand the caller at the same time. I have forgotten some of what the caller said, but not his last words.

"You meet Meester Roberts. Go to bank and get money."

I told him, "We can't get the bank open this time of night."

"Meester Roberts get bank open anytime he wants to. You do what I say. I know your grandsons. They be in danger. You can't watch all time."

Those last words terrified me. I called Karen, but as Carl wasn't at home, yet, I was afraid to tell her over the phone about what had just happened. I said I needed to come over and talk to Carl.

Karen said to come on, that Carl would be home shortly. I grabbed my keys, ran out of the house and drove straight over to see them. I pulled into their drive way, and went in through the garage door, without bothering to knock.

Carl had just gotten home. They were sitting in the den when I burst through the door. For a moment I stood there, shaking before I could get the words out, "The kidnapper's threatening to take the boys next!"

Karen jumped up, "What are you saying, Dad? What's happened?"

Taking me by the hand, she led me to a chair. "Sit down and tell us again."

I told them about the call, stammering, finding the words difficult to repeat.

Carl and Karen listened, but could hardly believe what they were hearing. Carl got up and called Allen at once. They agreed to get together the next morning and make plans for protecting the children.

Afterwards they sat up in the den most of the night. Karen and I were terrified for the boys, but Carl was also angry, enraged, outraged. He said more than once that night if he could get his hands on this monster, justice would be swift and sure.

The Perpetrator

Good. Good. You upright, God-fearing people! Worry about your children and your wives. Worry about what will happen if you don't see to it that I get the money. I need it. You'll be sorry if I don't get it, and soon.

Carl Johnson

The next morning Allen came early. We sat around the kitchen table and worked out what to do. Allen offered to hire guards for our oldest son, Cody, who was nine, and the only one who was apart from us for any length of time. Our other son was five and our daughter was only a baby. Cody, though, had to ride the bus to school.

I went to the school and met with the principal and Cody's teachers. They decided that someone would make sure the boy arrived safely on the bus every morning and got back on the bus every afternoon.

Karen Johnson

I had to be at work at the Post Office by 6:00 a.m. in nearby Oakland. That required me to leave before Carl and the kids even got up. I had never been afraid to drive by myself before, but there I was, on the road before dawn, and then I was afraid.

Carl Johnson

After Karen left for work, I would get up and if I had to leave early, I'd take the children down to my mother's house and Cody would catch the bus there. I had a talk with Cody and told him not to trust anyone—not a neighbor, not a policeman, not anyone.

We were doing a lot with the other parents at Cody's school, Chimney Rock Elementary. We'd built the outdoor classrooms for the kids, outdoor benches, and a gazebo. When they had Clean-up Day, I had to go and Cody had to come along with me. I wouldn't let him out of my sight.

There was no let up. When baseball season started it was so hard. A friend and I were in charge of the league. We had over 200 kids playing. We had to keep this going. We coached two or three teams each year. At the ballpark we had to make sure that we or someone was watching the kids every minute.

Karen Johnson

It was hard any evening when Carl had to be gone. At home, every time we heard the dog bark, we wondered if it was the kidnapper. The scary part is that, after a while, you get lax in spite of yourself, and then suddenly you're out somewhere and you lose sight of your kids. At that instant, for a moment that seems to stretch into an eternity, you are scared to death.

I had a rough time shopping with the baby and trying to keep up with Kyle, our five-year-old. We lived like this for months.

Mary Linda Rose

The church members never gave up looking for Doe. Mother and I began telling others that the caller had to be someone who knew the church members, or at least had one of the church directories.

We thought this because there are three Johnson children, the two boys and their baby girl. The pictures for the directory were done before the baby was born. The Johnson family picture only has Carl, Karen, and the two boys.

We would have done anything to find Doe. As it was, every time we drove to church we looked in the ditches for her body.

I decided that a friend of mine who was a psychic might help. I told Allen about this psychic friend and asked him to give me something of Doe's. He provided me with a blouse and some hair from her brush. This friend was going to do this for free, but her mother was critically ill at the time and we couldn't get together.

I'm the pianist at the church, and I try to get along with all the members, but I must say that Sylvia Lord and I were not friends. She made sure each Sunday to mention any mistakes I made playing the hymns.

When she and Charles joined the church, it didn't seem to matter what we had been doing before they came. From then on, as far as they were concerned, their way was the only way to do things.

I received a call from Sylvia one afternoon in March of 1993, which was strange even for Sylvia. My oldest daughter, Kristie, was in charge of the youth at the Church. Because of the threat to the Johnson children, she and I had made a pact that the children would not go anywhere without one of us. We had planned an outing that Sunday afternoon. Sylvia Lord said over the phone that she and Charles wanted to take the children instead of letting us do it.

I told her, "Well, Sylvia, we've already made arrangements and Kristie's going to supervise them this afternoon."

"No!" she said, her voice almost a shriek, "You don't understand. We've got to have the children this afternoon. We want to take them on that outing."

"Sylvia," I said, "we've made these plans. . ."

She interrupted me, "You all can go another day. We want to take the children today."

I stood firm, "Kristie's taking them. . . ."

"Well, Kristie can just have the day off!"

"Sylvia, those kids are going nowhere without Kristie. That's her job and they are her responsibility. Just forget it," I kept telling her, but she kept insisting that she and Charles were taking the children. She demanded that they didn't want any of us coming with them.

She stayed on the phone a long time arguing with me. She got really angry. I kept telling her this was not up for discussion.

By herself, Sylvia was usually a meek and mild woman who was generally pleasant enough. But when she was with

Charles and he let her know he wanted something, or for something to be done, she then became as demanding and overbearing as her husband.

About this same time, I arrived at work one day at Methodist Hospital North and learned that the FBI was watching me closely. A supervisor came up and asked, "Do you know Doe Roberts?"

"Yes," I replied. "She goes to my church and she's missing. You know, she's the one who made all those puppets for us to give the children."

"Well, the FBI has been here asking all these questions about you."

"Good," I said, "give them all the help you can."

Her voice became cautioning, as she said, "You don't understand. There were some phone calls made from here and they're looking at you."

I didn't think I had anything to fear. "Yes, I know. It's okay. Allen and I are friends. I know his sister Jean who stayed with him those first couple of months after Doe disappeared. Sometimes Allen would go out on the property walking or in his golf cart and Jean would get worried. She'd call me and we'd go looking for him."

Her voice became louder and less sympathetic. "You do not understand! The calls came from our lobby, and they've been asking if you were here the day they were made."

"That's crazy!" I couldn't believe what I heard.

After that, another person came up to me and told me the same thing. That's how we found out that some of the calls were made from the hospital.

Miriam Foley

I never gave up on Doe coming back. I knew the

Roberts' marriage was a good one. I had never heard Doe criticize Allen or say anything negative about him. Even after they retired, I knew Allen wanted to and tried to meet Doe for lunch every day.

Yet knowing all this, I decided that the only answer, for whatever reason, was that Doe had run away. I clung to this belief to the end. Many times on my two mile walk down Great Oaks Road and through the Wildwood neighborhood I would play these scenarios over and over in my mind, thinking, "Doe please come home. It doesn't matter what's wrong. Just come home."

Often my daughter, on visits from Nashville, would admonish me to come to grips with the fact that Doe had to be dead. I always refused. I would not give up on the possibility that my friend would return.

Another thing my daughter kept saying was that the caller had to be someone in the church. At first, I also refused to listen to this, until the day I heard one of the tapes made by Ron Cline. I thought I recognized the voice as belonging to Charles Lord.

I told Karen Johnson that I thought I knew who it was. When Karen demanded to know, I refused to say anything more. I just couldn't believe that it really was Charles or that he could do such a thing.

Karen let me take the tape. I listened to the tape over and over again. I couldn't believe it myself, but after listening for so long, I became convinced that the voice was Charles Lord.

Malinda Lancaster

I had not heard from the kidnapper since the calls the previous December. Sylvia Lord and I had not been close before, but since the kidnapping, Sylvia had made it a practice to drop in on me, ask me what I had heard, and in general talk about Doe. I knew from Sylvia that FBI agents were regular callers at the Lords' home. I was invited to one of these sessions.

One afternoon Jo Anne called and told me to come down to the Lords'. The FBI had run out of clues and Jo Anne recently had been to Quantico to review tactics. I sat down around the table with Charles, Sylvia, Jo Anne, and Ramona to brainstorm and see if we could remember anything that would help. I'm not sure exactly what the date was, but I remember Charles' azaleas were blooming and thinking how pretty they were.

Later that evening, Sylvia called me to ask if Lon and I would like to go with them to Ryan's Steak House for dinner. Sylvia said she had been given a blood test that morning and told me she needed to eat a steak. We had not ever done anything socially with them before, but as the meeting had run so long, no one had cooked dinner. They picked us up and we rode over to Bartlett for steak.

Charles has a strange personality and it seemed that Sylvia always tried not to cross him. During that evening, and at most times as I recall, Charles tried to dominate everyone, especially Sylvia.

The FBI

While the Lancasters and the Lords were having dinner, the law enforcement agents had plans of their own.

Allen

One afternoon late in March of 1993, I received a telephone call from FBI agent Jo Anne Overall. She said, "Mr. Roberts, there's been a new development in the case. Can you come talk with us?"

"Us" must have meant Ramona would be with Jo Anne.

Her voice was matter-of-fact, no real emotion in it, so I figured they hadn't found Doe or her kidnapper. Still, she piqued my curiosity. I asked, "When and where?"

She hesitated a moment before answering, "At the Shoney's restaurant in Germantown. You know where it is, don't you?"

I told her I did.

"We'll see you there around seven this evening, if that's okay with you? I'll call you there if anything comes up to prevent us from making it."

I said, "See you then."

* * *

I arrived promptly at seven o'clock and took a seat in a booth, where I ordered a cup of coffee with creamer and sweetener and waited for the detectives to arrive. The minutes dragged on, into half an hour, then an hour.

It was unlike Jo Anne to be tardy, but I assumed the development she had mentioned must have been a big one and was causing this delay.

After two hours I became nervous and concerned. Why hadn't they showed up or called yet? If she knew this place, she must also know the telephone number like she indicated. It seemed pretty inconsiderate that she had not yet called. Her lack of consideration chafed me.

A little after 9:30 I heard the phone ring. A waitress came over to me and asked, "Are you Allen Roberts?"

I indicated I was.

"Phone's for you."

It was Jo Anne. "Allen, I'm sorry to call so late and make you wait so long. Can you meet us at the Holiday Inn on Poplar just west of the expressway?"

"I guess so. What do I do and where do I go when I get there?"

"One of us will meet you in the lobby."

Before leaving, I tried to telephone Bill Simmons, but didn't get an answer. So I called Ron Cline, told him where I was going, and to call Bill. I said, "Tell him that if he doesn't hear from me by one o'clock, to come and rescue me."

* * *

The person who met me was Ramona Swain. She is a large woman, not fat, but stocky—more like a man as far as her physical contours looked to me. She greeted me in a business-like manner, shook my hand, then ushered me onto an elevator that took us to the fifth floor.

Jo Anne Overall was waiting inside the room. Both women were dressed in dark suit dresses. After greeting me, Jo Anne became all business. She motioned for me to sit on one of the double beds. Once I did, she and Ramona sat across from me on the other bed. Both stared intensely at me, their faces otherwise expressionless.

"Mr. Roberts," Jo Anne began, "our case histories show that, more than nine times out of ten, when a married woman disappears her husband is the one responsible."

I took a deep breath and swallowed, realizing they'd lured me here so they could interrogate me.

Responding to Jo Anne, I said, "You're telling me I just spent nearly three hours drinking coffee at Shoney's waiting for you to inform me about some 'important development,' but it was only so you could lure me here and let you badger me?" I hoped my edginess wasn't obvious.

She looked over at Ramona, then back at me. "I wouldn't call it 'badgering.' We're doing our job. We want to *question* you. Since we first interviewed you, we really have not reviewed the details of the case with you."

I asked what "details" did she mean?

Ramona stepped in, "You were the last person to see your wife alive."

Keeping calm, I said, "That's correct."

"That fact alone makes you a suspect. . . our *prime suspect*."

My anger swelled, but I knew better than to lose it. These were professional law enforcement personnel trained to do their work a certain way, and they were doing it. For me to get mad would not do me any good. It might even make me look guilty, something I certainly didn't want and could not afford to let happen.

I restrained myself and tried to appeal to their logic. "Doe was my wife and best friend of forty-four years. What motive would I have to get rid of her? I loved her. What could I possibly gain?

They were quiet for a few seconds. Then Ramona resumed, "We have no other leads at this time. We've followed every lead anyone had to offer, but they all came up dead ends. Everything seems to point back to you."

"It may look that way to you," I said, "but that's not how it is."

Ramona's jaw jutted out as she said, "We recently were contacted by what we feel is a reliable outside source who swears you are the guilty person. We're prepared to follow up with whatever it takes to prove you are the culprit." Her voice was not threatening, just a matter-of-fact tone with the authority one would expect from a seasoned detective.

I shook my head and said, "I don't care who tells you what, I know that I am telling you the truth." Who on earth was that "outside source" and why would they tease me with that?

Jo Anne said, "We did a background check on you.

Didn't find a lot, but one item caught our attention. It looks like you seriously understated an income source on a prior year's income tax return. Do you remember that?"

She gave me the additional details.

I said, "I thought it was an aggressive position, but not an illegal one. Are you telling me otherwise?"

Ramona responded, "Yes. And I'm sure you can see where that goes—a man who would cheat on his taxes might also cheat on and get rid of his wife."

That remark stung me to my heart. No doubt they were referring to Esther. Good, innocent Esther. I had lost Doe and found Esther, and they were hammering away at me using both women. But I ignored her and told Jo Anne I would file an amended return right away.

Taking a quick mental inventory, I had learned that evening that I was now the prime suspect, they had an "outside source" to prove me guilty, and that I had understated a major item of income on an income tax return. All circumstantial evidence. All speculative, but enough to turn them away from seeking out the real culprit and focus on me.

It went back and forth like that for some time. At almost one o'clock in the morning I began to feel weak and started trembling. I asked, "May I have something to eat? I haven't had anything for several hours."

Jo Anne picked up the phone and ordered something. A few minutes later someone arrived with a cold can of Coca-Cola and a Snickers candy bar. I quickly consumed both and began to feel my strength return slowly. I telephoned Bill Simmons and told him I was all right and not to worry about me.

The two female agents waited a few more minutes, then Jo Anne resumed. "Mr. Roberts, I hope you understand that we are just doing our job. We don't have anything personal against you. We have followed every lead that's come up, but they don't take us anywhere. You were the last person we know of who saw Doe alive. That—and the fact you are her husband—makes you the prime suspect. I wish it wasn't so, but that's how things stand."

Once more I fought to remain calm and not take offense at her words, reminding myself anger would only weaken my defenses. But I was growing tired of this "cat-and-mouse" game.

I stood up and looked at my watch. It was a quarter until two a.m.

"I'm tired and want to go home now."

Ramona said, "You realize we could have you brought into custody to continue this questioning, don't you?"

I replied, "You are free to do whatever you think is your duty. You know where I live. I'm not going to leave town or skip the country, or do anything like that because I know I'm innocent. But if you wouldn't mind, I'd like to go home now."

Jo Anne nodded to Ramona and said, "It is late. Let's call it a night."

I rode down the elevator and walked out to the parking lot. When I started the Volkswagen, I don't know why, but for some reason I headed out the driveway that led to the westbound lane of Poplar Avenue which went toward downtown Memphis instead of going out the driveway on the south end of the property which would have led me heading east toward home.

Later on Jo Anne told me they had sent someone to follow me, but because I went the opposite direction of what they expected, I immediately lost their "tail."

Bill Simmons

By 1:15 a.m. Bill had become infuriated and was about to rush over to pick up Allen when his uncle called. Allen also sounded angry and, by that time, somewhat confused in his description of what the women had asked him.

The next day, while Bill was at the auto parts store, one of the male FBI agents came by. Bill explained to him that they should not be calling his uncle out at night like that again. If they decided they needed an audience with Allen, Bill would also have to be present. The agent said that Bill couldn't do that, but Bill informed him that he had Allen's power of attorney and that's the way it would be.

The agent was 5'7" and barely came up to Bill's chest. He apparently understood that Bill was not to be trifled with at that moment and decided not to press the issue.

Allen

The kidnapper-caller apparently decided that harassing the neighbors and family wasn't enough. On March 4th, he had made a call to Joe Birch at WMC television station and told him that Doe was dead. Birch taped the conversation, and after talking with the FBI, aired the tape on the evening news. Thousands of people then got to hear that sickening voice called "Charlie Chan".

Over the next few weeks he called the station several more times. The next time he contradicted himself and said Doe was alive, but she would need protection *from her husband* for a year. I knew Doe had no need of protection! We began to think the caller was truly deranged.

I was fighting several battles at once: The constant watchfulness for the Johnson children, the bizarre and senseless calls from the kidnapper, and the weight of suspicion from the investigators, old friends and even some family members. Doe's sisters were distant and cold, and my sisters, Willy and Jean, were critical of my friendship with Esther.

On March 19, 1993, a Federal Grand Jury convened in Shelby County to review the case. Esther and two other women I had had dinner with were called to testify, along with Brenda Keith and some other square dance friends. They were placed under oath and could not reveal their testimony.

I was not called. From my absence, I had to infer that Jo Anne and Ramona were trying to get an indictment against me. The Grand Jury reviewed the case again on April 1st, but no indictment was handed down.

This had no effect on the caller, who continued his relentless campaign. His next targets were Ann and Gus Richmond, not long after WMC ran their first news story that March.

Ann Richmond

For months I thought that the kidnapper would leave Doe inside the church, tied and gagged to a chair or worse. My greatest fear was of discovering Doe's body discarded there for some hapless church member to find.

Most Sundays I was the first person at church. Each week I parked and went up the steps with small whispers of fear inside my head. Each week I opened the door slowly, looked carefully before stepping inside and paused to listen. Sometimes I called out, "Doe?"

Week after week I searched every inch of the church—the kitchen and Recreation Hall, checking both sides of the old upright piano on the east wall, looking under the tables and in the corners formed by the two accordion room dividers. Then climbing up the steps into the sanctuary, walking down the aisle, slowly looking under every pew on either side. In front of the altar, I turned to the right to look in the vestibule, past the pulpit, whose door opened out to the parking lot. Next I turned and walked to the other side of the small sanctuary and stepped behind the piano to look in the storeroom to the left of the pulpit.

The door to this storage room was kept open at the insistence of Charles Lord because of the stained glass window that filled the back wall. Shelves lined the space beneath the window and rose to shoulder height on both sides. Christmas decorations, old Sunday school books, wreaths, candles, the usual accumulation from church activities were stored there, some neatly, some in a jumble on the shelves. Every element of this room was familiar, but there wasn't any comfort in that familiarity. Doe wasn't there.

In early May I received a call—the call from which I hoped I would be spared. Gus usually sat by the phone. The caller made several attempts, but Gus could not understand him and hung up on him. The last time he called, the strange voice demanded to speak to "Miss Ann."

"Just a minute," my husband said, then brought the phone to me.

I had been relaxing, watching television. I picked up the portable phone from Gus and put it to my ear. Then he tells me my eyes grew large, as my fingers gripped the phone, and I saw my knuckles suddenly become as white as the short hair combed back behind my ears.

I recognized the voice immediately having just heard it on TV a few days before. Because I was on a portable phone it was hard for me to hear or understand him. I kept repeating, "I can't hear you. I can't hear you."

He kept getting louder and louder, making his demand. He finally got across to me that he wanted me to make Allen pay the ransom. I told him that I didn't even know where Allen was, nor could I contact Allen. I was telling the kidnapper the truth. It was my understanding that Allen was not staying at his home in Eads at that time. The kidnapper kept insisting that I call Allen. I told him again I couldn't.

I was so unnerved by that call. I thought about what I should do and decided to call Carl Johnson. I knew he would know how to reach Allen and the FBI. Carl gave me Jo Anne's number.

Before I could call Jo Anne, the phone rang. It was my daughter, Mary Linda, calling from New Orleans.

Mary Linda Rose

I still can't get over the coincidence of phoning my mother just after the kidnapper had called. I had visited a psychic to ask about Doe. The woman told me Doe was still alive and being held south by southwest. She also told me that her kidnapping had something to do with the church. Well I wanted to call mother with this glimmer of good news immediately. When she answered I could tell she was upset and understandably so when she told me the kidnapper had just called.

I asked, "Have you called the FBI?"

"Not yet. I just got the number from Carl. I was getting ready to call when you phoned."

I said, "Mother you sound so upset. Maybe I should come home tonight."

"No, this is more of the same thing that's been happening to the others. I'll be okay"

Ann Richmond

I hung up after talking with Mary Linda and called Jo Anne Overall. Jo Anne thanked me and said that if they needed me they would get back in touch, but she never called me.

About ten minutes later, Sylvia Lord called, saying, "I understand you have gotten a call from the kidnapper. How are you feeling? I know it's distressing. I know it's upsetting."

I should have asked her how she knew about that, but the thought escaped me. Instead, I said, "Yes, it is very upsetting. I really do appreciate you calling, Sylvia." I was so rattled I didn't question how she might have known.

By this time it was after 10:00. Even though Carl had given us Allen's number, I didn't want to call Allen that late at night. I phoned him the next morning and told him about the call. He thanked me and said how much he appreciated it, especially since there were those who did not let him know when things happened.

Mary Linda Rose

After I came back from New Orleans, Mother and I went to church and were talking about the psychic. Charles came walking up, catching the last few words of our conversation. He demanded, "What's going on?"

I said, "I've spoken with a psychic who says Doe is alive, that she's being held somewhere south by southwest, and that the church was connected with the kidnapping."

Charles became all nervous, "Yes, yes. There's—there's a cult in Helena, Arkansas."

The next Sunday Charles came up to me after church and flashed a badge, then quickly put it away and said, "I've been authorized to take any information. You have to come with me so that I can talk to you."

Unimpressed and unintimidated, I quickly responded, "I'm not going anywhere with you, Charles. You can just forget that."

"No," he insisted, "you have to come with me now!"

"I don't care who's authorized you or what you say. I'm not going anywhere with you, Charles. You can just forget that!"

Even though Charles was adamant, I didn't give in. I don't have any respect for a badge. You can buy those at any pawn shop. I was not going to the parking lot to talk to Charles Lord.

I told him that I wasn't going to talk to him, not about anything. I would talk to the FBI, but not to him. Later on I did have a phone conversation with Jo Anne, and later with Agent Chuck Daley about what the psychic had told me. Daley insisted on giving me his phone number in case anything came up.

When Charles said something to me again, I told him I was dealing with Jo Anne Overall and Chuck Daley.

"What are you doing talking to them?" Charles asked in a sharp tone.

"Never you mind," I told him and walked away. He didn't like that.

* * *

From *The Commercial Appeal*, May 1, 1993:

FBI SEEKS CALLER TO TV STATION

Source: Chris Conley.

FBI officials again are asking a man who called a local television station claiming to have information about the disappearance of Martha 'Doe' Roberts to contact them directly. "Our primary concern is with the welfare of Doe Roberts," said Robert Wright, special agent in charge of the Memphis FBI office. "We will do whatever it takes to assure her safe return."

'Doe' Roberts, 65, was last seen Aug. 7 by her husband Allen C. Roberts at their 150-acre spread near Eads.

A federal grand jury investigation into the disappearance commenced last month.

* * *

On April 29th, WMC Channel 5 aired another taped demand from the caller, who said, "Deliver $100,000, the money in tens and twenties, to Lancaster man or Lord man by noon tomorrow."

Agent Jo Anne Overall

The next night Jo Anne Overall asked Charles Lord to deliver a statement on WMC. In it he asked the caller to please contact the FBI directly.

On May 4, Allen met with Ramona and Jo Anne. They told him that the latest ransom payment had not been met because the caller could not give enough information about Doe. Jo Anne instructed Allen to keep in touch with them as to his whereabouts. They warned him not to make any investigations on his own as anything he turned up would be suspect.

Allen Roberts

That most recent meeting with the investigators began a long period of hoping against hope.

CHAPTER FOURTEEN

In the summer of 1993, several people began to come to the same conclusion. As in the parable of "The Sower and the Seed," some rejected what they discovered.

Ann Richmond

One Sunday after church, I was standing in the aisle talking with a group. Charles was there and I asked him, "What kind of person would do those things? He must be *insane.*"

Tapping his forehead with his forefinger, Charles said, "Well, I don't know, but he's *very smart.*"

Sometimes Miriam Foley and I would stay and talk about Doe after church, when everyone else was gone. One Sunday in June, Miriam said, "I want to talk." So we sat down in the back of the church.

I said, "Let's put all these facts on a piece of paper."

I drew out a matrix. I'm a math supervisor for the Board of Education and have used this technique many times as a classroom exercise. We put everybody's name on it that had a connection to the case; most of whom were church members. We thought of all the things that had taken place —telephone calls, trips to meet the kidnapper, sightings—everything we could think of, and cross-referenced them. We eliminated names one by one. When we got through, we examined our matrix. Only one name had an 'X' in every category—Charles Lord.

Miriam had talked with her daughter in Nashville many times about this case. Constantly, in fact. She told me Pam kept telling her it had to be someone in the church. Miriam would come back and tell us this, and we would say, "No way!" That day when we sat there in the back pew looking at the matrix, we still said, 'This can't be right. Not Charles, not Charles Lord!'

Miriam said, 'I want to take this home and show it to Tim."

Several weeks later I asked her about it, and she said they had thrown that thing away. We didn't tell anyone else.

Miriam Foley

It's hard to explain. It was like a shroud covering our eyes.

Ann Richmond

We knew the FBI suspected Allen. We talked about this all the time. Sometimes in Sunday school class, when we didn't have lessons, we talked. Some of our members, especially Hazel and Doris wouldn't allow any discussion in their presence. We respected both of them, but if they weren't in Sunday school, we talked. We wondered why the FBI never questioned any of us, though they had gone back to the Johnsons several times, accusing Allen. Carl and Karen kept telling them there was no way Allen could be guilty, but the investigators didn't listen.

The Knox Family Becomes More Involved

In the last week of May, the Knoxes—William Paul, Larry, Jane, and Patty—became concerned about their mother Jewell. The year had taken its toll on Doe's younger sister, who insisted on believing that Doe was still alive, against all odds. Jewell had dreamed of Doe dancing at the foot of her bed, beckoning her sister to come and find her.

The Knoxes held a family gathering over at William Paul's paint store in Olive Branch, Mississippi. Different family members had taped the news reports which they watched again while having dinner. One of the reports shocked William Paul.

As sharp as William Paul Knox is, he admits to having missed that clue. That day was the first time Charles Lord claimed Doe had called him because Allen wouldn't help her. It had to be a lie. If his Aunt Doe needed help, and Allen couldn't or wouldn't help her, William Paul knew she would have called a close family member, not Charles Lord. He had to be lying. It just hit him in the face. He wrote down that day Charles Lord was the kidnapper.

So they decided to set a trap. They started with Larry carrying their Momma and Aunt Viola over to the Lords' house for a visit. They wanted to do two things: first, for Lord to know that Doe's family could pay the ransom and, second, to give him a telephone number that couldn't be found any other way except by their having given it to him.

Larry and William Paul did not tell their mother about their suspicions of Lord, nor of their plans.

Jewell Knox

I didn't know we were going to the Lords' until after we got in the car and drove up to Eads. We were at Olive Branch the day we went to see Charles Lord. I had broken my foot and had a cast on my leg, up above the knee. Larry had called Charles Lord and said we wanted to come out and talk to him about Doe. Charles met us at a store in Eads, and then we followed him to his house.

Charles showed us around his yard and called particular attention to his roses. He was real proud of his garden. He pointed to all the plants that Doe had given them, some that

117

she had set out herself. As I hobbled around on my crutches, there was this one fenced-in place in the backyard, and when I noticed it, cold chills just covered me.

We had sat down in the living room when I saw Jo Anne and Ramona drive up. Charles said that he didn't think we'd mind if they were present. I told him no, we didn't, since I had talked with them lots a times.

The women agents came in and sat down on the couch, Larry sat next to them. I sat in a chair in the corner. Viola was seated next to the kitchen door.

I remember one of them, Ramona, trying to talk about Allen having lots of girl friends—before Doe went missing.

Larry laughed out loud and said, "A girlfriend? A.C. Roberts? Why Doe would have clawed his eyes out!"

While we talked, Jo Anne and Ramona were busy writing down everything we said.

I asked Charles, when did he talk to Doe? He said that he talked with her on January the third, after she went missing in August.

I asked him, "Well, what did she tell you?"

He said she told him that Allen wouldn't pay the ransom so she could come home. We told Charles then, that if Allen wouldn't pay, that we would.

We stayed about forty-five minutes. Charles didn't say much, but Sylvia never stopped talking. She told us how she and Doe had done so many things together.

We left before Jo Anne and Ramona. Sylvia Lord walked us out to the car. She asked us for a phone number. Larry gave her his work number, as well as his unlisted home number.

William Paul Knox and Larry Knox's Plan

William Paul wasn't quite prepared for the impression the Lords made on his mother and aunt.

After the visit, they came back to the shop. Their mother was impressed with Charles Lord. She was convinced he was innocent and said she thought William Paul was crazy to suspect Lord.

Jewell Knox

The very next day, June 8, 1993, I got a call from the kidnapper. He said if I wanted my sister back to bring $100,000 to a motel at the Canada Road exit on I-40. I was to stay in the motel room, and Larry was to come to the telephone at the Outlet Mall at 8:00 that night. He said no police. Then, as I later found out, he called Larry—at the unlisted number we had given to Sylvia Lord.

The Knox Brothers Take Action

When Larry answered the phone, a man's voice with a heavy Oriental accent asked, "Are you nephew of woman Martha Doe Roberts?"

Larry answered that he was and asked the man if he had his aunt.

The caller said, "I want to talk about woman."

Larry asked if his aunt was okay.

"Woman okay. You listen, I talk.

"Woman say you must first promise not to tell Roberts man about this phone call. He cannot be trusted. He refuse to pay me what he owes me. He will not pay the ransom."

Larry promised, and then asked again about Doe.

"Woman okay. You listen, I talk. Roberts man promised to pay me hundred thousand dollars. He has refused. He has called FBI. He has called police. He is not trusted.

"Woman in bad shape. Needs medicine. Will not last much longer. You pay me. I let you have woman."

Larry told the caller he couldn't raise a hundred thousand dollars, but he could raise a good deal of money.

The caller then asked, "Can you make seventy-five thousand dollars?"

Larry said he might, but would need more time. He also asked how the caller obtained his telephone number.

"I ask questions. You answer. I know all about you. You make plenty money. You rich. Do you want to see woman alive?"

Larry replied that he did, but did not think he could raise so much money on such short notice. He said he would try, though.

"You know Factory Outlet Store on I-40?"

He said he did.

"You be at Factory Outlet Store tomorrow at 12 noon. Wait there at front entrance by phone booth. Bring money. I will give you woman for money. Okay?"

Larry agreed to be there.

"Okay," said the voice and hung up.

Larry then called to his wife, Carolyn, and told her he had just talked to his Aunt Doe's kidnapper, accent and everything.

It was Tuesday, June 8, 1993, and the time 10:00 a.m. Larry and Carolyn lived in Rutherford, Tennessee, where they ran a used car business. They lived on the premises in an apartment in back of the sales office.

He told Carolyn the kidnapper wanted him to come up

with $75,000 and take it to the Factory Outlet Mall the next day.

She told him he would have to call his brother William Paul and get his help because they did not have enough money by themselves.

Larry made the calls, first to William Paul, then to their mother. It was hard to believe her sister, Martha Doe Roberts, had been missing now ten months.

Larry drove to Olive Branch, Mississippi, and met William Paul at his paint store to discuss what needed to be done and how to do it. Leonard Jones, their uncle who was Doe's brother, was also brought in, and they decided how to raise the money demanded by "Charley Chan."

The people in the Eads community had given the kidnapper that name because of the accent of the anonymous caller, and then the news people picked up on it, too. He became known as "Charley Chan."

The Knox brothers planned to be at the Factory Outlet Mall at the appointed time with the money as promised. They decided to embellish on the plan both for safety's sake and to entrap Charley Chan if they could.

William Paul would arrive separately and walk the Mall pretending to shop, staying in a position to help Larry if it became necessary. Only members of the Jones and Knox families would know about this. Allen Roberts and the FBI would not be included.

At a couple of minutes before noon on Wednesday, June 9, Larry entered the Factory Outlet Mall through the south entrance, walked straight through to the phone booths, found a seat on a nearby bench and sat down to wait.

At ten minutes past noon, according to their plan, William Paul parked his car in the west side parking lot and entered through the west entrance. He proceeded to walk the halls as planned, pretending to shop, while keeping a watch on everyone and looking for anything suspicious. He knew it would be hard not to call attention to himself. Others had always told him he stood out.

Although only of medium build, he is muscular and wiry from years of hard physical work and exercise, and his presence in a confrontation would be threatening. He has a full head of curly, sandy colored hair, which makes him look younger than his middle age. Dark glasses were of little disguise, being inside the mall, so he took them off.

* * *

They checked into the motel about 3:00 p.m. that day. They didn't want the room with the money in it to be empty while they were gone, so Uncle Leonard remained stationed there, while the Knox brothers went to the Mall and found a secluded place to watch the phone booth.

Larry waited by the phone over at the Mall, as instructed, but nothing happened. They waited several hours, then returned to the motel, spent the night, and then went back to work the next day.

After that first failed attempt, they figured it was just a hoax. But before Larry made it back home that day to Rutherford, the kidnapper called Larry's wife. The game was still on and they knew then they were players.

* * *

As the Knox brothers made their rounds in the mall, they both felt a rush of excitement from the sense of danger and urgency. Both were ready to take on Doe's kidnapper or killer, and either would have given his life for her. This was the first real break they'd had.

Thoughts flooded William Paul's memory about how Aunt Doe had always been so close to them. Right then, he could remember how she'd take his hand as a little boy and they'd go walking. He could look up at her face and feel her confidence in herself, which made him feel the same way about himself for the rest of his life. That was his gift from Aunt Doe and he loved her for it. If Aunt Doe needed help, and couldn't call Uncle Allen, William Paul believed she would've called him then, if she could.

William Paul would pass by Larry and carefully act as though he was ignoring him. On his second pass, he noticed two large and apparently suspicious men, and followed them for a while. But then they finally made a purchase and left the mall, indicating his suspicions had been misplaced.

Larry would change his lookout position from time to time, trying to be as inconspicuous as possible. Several times the security guard would stop and speak to him. After about two hours, a clerk, then a passer-by spoke to him, asking what his business was in the mall. He gave the excuse that he was waiting on his wife. Larry admits that he felt and probably acted nervous for two good reasons—he had two guns concealed on his person and seventy-five thousand dollars in his shoes.

This went on for about four hours, until William Paul gave him the sign to give up and go home.

While Larry and his brother William Paul were occupied outside of Memphis, Carolyn had stayed behind in Rutherford to run the used car lot. About eleven that morning she received a phone call from Charley Chan.

He said, "This is Carol, wife of Larry man?"

She acknowledged the fact and asked who he was.

"You be quiet. I talk. You listen. You tell Larry bring money to Days Inn Hotel at Canada Road and I-40. Tell Larry bring money and his mama. Tell Larry to bring comb and brush and clean clothes and medicine for Roberts woman. She in bad shape. She need medicine. You got pencil and paper?"

She told him she was ready.

"You keep quiet. I talk. Write names and phone numbers when I give them. Ronald Cline, phone number 555-3441; Carl Johnson, 555-6499; Charles Lord, 555-8650; Tim Foley, 555-3446. When you call these persons, you ask them what they know about Roberts woman. One will know; and you will find out how to get woman back."

After these instructions the caller hung up. She sat there, stunned. Thoughts were racing through her mind so fast they made her dizzy. She realized Charley Chan had tricked Larry and had lured him to the mall, then not showed up. He had guessed she'd be at the car lot to take the call, not Larry. This could be another set-up, so what should she do?

Was Aunt Doe still alive? Could her Larry get himself killed? Would they lose all their savings? Would Larry end up killing somebody and getting himself charged with murder?

After sitting and thinking for a few minutes, she poured herself a cup of coffee, sat down and tried to calm her feelings.

She picked up the phone and called her mother-in-law Jewell Knox, Aunt Doe's sister.

Jewell Knox

After Carolyn called me that morning and told me about the telephone conversation she'd had with Charley Chan, I phoned my daughter, Jane Brown, in Olive Branch. Jane worked for William Paul Knox in the house painting and building part of his business. She paged William Paul on his beeper, and he went right to a pay phone and returned her call. She passed on what I heard from Carolyn and told him, then called me back to let me know he had the information.

William Paul and Larry quit their posts at the Mall for the day. Larry returned to Rutherford and William Paul to Olive Branch. After a flurry of calls among Larry, William Paul, Uncle Leonard, Jewell, and other family members, they decided to rendezvous that evening at the Days Inn and do exactly as Charley Chan had specified. . . with one exception.

Jewell Knox, age 67, would not attend. William Paul would take her place. Uncle Leonard and his nephew-in-law, Ray Dunn, would arm themselves and get a room next door to the one occupied by the Knox brothers. At that point they were confident of their ability to meet all of the kidnapper's demands, and, all things being equal, it now looked like they would get their Aunt Doe back.

The Knox brothers had not notified the FBI about the mall rendezvous. Everything was happening so fast, during daylight hours, and they were trying to follow directions exactly. They didn't trust the law enforcement officials any longer. Nothing had gone right in this case.

Resentment toward the detectives was widespread among them. But, by this time it would be night. Confrontation, with its attendant danger, was now a greater possibility. At this time they felt they needed and wanted all the help they could get, and were willing to ask for it.

Larry called Jo Anne Overall and told her about the phone call he had received on Tuesday morning, then about the Wednesday stake-out at the mall, and finally the plans for the second meeting at Days Inn within a few hours. Jo Anne pitched a fit that all this had happened without her being informed in advance. She told him he had not given her enough time to prepare for the meeting they had scheduled for that night, saying they would have to operate on their own without FBI backup. She asked him to keep her informed about the outcome.

William Paul broke in on the conversation and complained to her that the FBI was not giving them any backup and still it wanted them to tell them everything that happened. In an angry voice he demanded that they would tell the FBI what happened, provided the agents would tell the Knox brothers what evidence the agency had against their uncle, Allen Roberts.

Jo Anne agreed. She explained that, number one, their uncle was the last person to admit to seeing his wife alive, and, number two, statistically, the husband is usually the killer.

Larry asked what motive did she suppose Allen had for committing such a crime?"

Jo Anne responded the motives were money, infidelity, fighting with his spouse.

Larry inquired which of those was she trying to pin on Uncle Allen?

She replied that they were still working on it.

William Paul and Larry had to make a few alterations in their plans. Because of her age and the potential danger, there was no way they were going to let their mother accompany them.

Larry, Uncle Leonard, Ray Dunn, and William Paul arrived at the Days Inn Motel in Lakeland at 7 p.m. on Thursday, June 10th. They had made reservations for two adjoining rooms on the second floor. Larry and William Paul took room 215, Uncle Leonard and his nephew the one next door, 217.

At eight p.m. Larry made his first phone call. It was to Ronald Cline. He identified himself as a nephew of Doe Roberts and said he was told that Ron had some information about her.

Cline responded, "No, I don't have anything to tell you. I don't know you. If I had anything to tell, I would call Allen

Roberts and tell him."

Larry's next call was to Carl Johnson. He again identified himself as a nephew of Doe Roberts and said Carl's name and phone number were given to him along with the suggestion that Carl had some information about Larry's aunt.

Carl said, "No, I have already told the FBI all I know. I don't have any idea why anyone would give you my number. What is this anyway?"

Larry later came to realize that Carl had already been badgered by Jo Anne and her assistant Chuck Daley, who seemed pretty good at threatening people with "obstruction of justice." Carl and his wife Karen had already had their feelings ruffled in this manner, and Larry's call only added more of the same.

The next name on the list was Charles Lord. Larry dialed the number and then waited.

"Hello," said a voice.

Larry asked if it was Charles Lord.

"Yes, it is."

Larry identified himself and asked Lord if he remembered him, reminding Lord how he and his family had stopped by the Lords' house last month. He then said he was told that Lord might have some information about Doe to share with him.

Lord said, "Yes, I do, but we can't talk over the phone. My phone is bugged. We'll have to meet somewhere. Where are you?"

Larry told Lord he was at the Days Inn on Canada Road, in Room 215. Did Lord know where that was?

He did and said he would come right over.

They hadn't told Jo Anne or Ramona about that first

meeting they had scheduled. William Paul wouldn't let Larry call them. By then William Paul was convinced that Charles was an informer to the FBI, maybe a paid informant, or perhaps worse. If he wasn't, then he was playing the agents like a violin.

* * *

Charles Lord came to the room. When he entered he was tense and argumentative, demanding to know if they were wired. Was the room bugged? Had they called the FBI?

They told Lord to look around, see for himself that they were on their own and alone. After a few minutes he settled down and started telling them that Doe was a wonderful lady and how much he cared for her. He said how sorry Allen was not to pay the ransom demands. He asked if the Knoxes were prepared to meet the kidnapper's demands and what had they brought with them.

William Paul answered for them, saying they came prepared to take Doe back. He then questioned Charles Lord about the rumors that Uncle Allen had done this. This seemed to upset Charles, and he raved on about how Allen didn't want her back. Then he asked if they had brought the money.

When William Paul asked how Lord knew about the money, he said not to play games. Lord grew belligerent, as though he was trying to scare them. Next, he said that William Paul was not supposed to be there, that Doe's sister, Jewell, was supposed to be there instead. That really caught the Knox brothers' attention.

When they asked him how he knew Jewell was supposed to be there, he jumped up and went crazy, stomping around, pacing. He denied having said that, and asked who was William Paul, anyway? He kept denying he had made the statement about Jewell.

William Paul and Larry kept telling Lord they were only

there to take Doe home. Did he have anything for them? If not, what was he doing there? Charles acted like he was getting ready to explode. He seemed wired out to the limit on nervous energy.

Charles said, "Larry has the money, right?"

They neither confirmed nor denied Lord's statement. It was obvious he believed that Larry had the money on him. He kept saying they needed to change locations, and "Let's go." He really wanted to go somewhere else. He kept asking Larry to go with him. But there was no way William Paul was going to let that happen.

About that time the phone rang. Larry answered and pretended to be talking to his wife. William Paul knew it couldn't be her and realized that Larry must have informed Jo Anne and Ramona about this meeting—and that it must be them on the phone. William Paul opened the door and went out on the balcony.

Charles followed him, still upset, and they got into a shoving match. Charles' shirt tore, and he fell down the steps. During the course of their altercation, William Paul's shirt also came open and Charles Lord saw William Paul was carrying a .38 in a waist holster. Lord's eyes grew wide.

He went to his truck, but then came back. The Knox brothers were watching him the entire time from the balcony. He tried once more to persuade Larry to come with him, saying, "If you have the money, I think I can contact the kidnapper."

Finally, William Paul told him, "I've got the money, but nobody is going with you. Not anywhere."

He left and didn't come back. After that, the Knoxes left, too.

Larry told William Paul that Jo Anne and Ramona said in their phone call they were parked down the road where they could watch the room. The Knox brothers drove to meet them.

William Paul pulled up on the driver's side, where Ramona was seated. She told him to get out; they wanted to know what had happened. William Paul told her he wasn't getting out of the car until he had driven it back to Mississippi. If they wanted to talk, they could follow.

When they crossed the state line, William Paul pulled over and then they talked. He recounted what had happened and said Charles Lord had to be the kidnapper.

Ramona said he was wrong.

William Paul begged them at least to run a credit check on Lord. He said that Lord was too preoccupied with money. Something was out of whack in Lord's life and it would show up if the investigators looked.

Ramona was so sure his Uncle Allen was guilty that she brushed off everything.

Finally, William Paul bet her a three hundred dollar steak dinner that Charles Lord was guilty.

Ramona replied that she would take that bet.

When the Knoxes left the investigators, they were still convinced that the brothers were wrong. However, by 7:30 the next morning, Jo Anne and Ramona had a different attitude.

Jo Anne called, asking William Paul some serious questions about Charles. William Paul thought, because of what he and his brother suggested, the law enforcement agents had found something in bank records that made them start looking seriously at Charles as a suspect for the first time.

Tommy Fullen

During June, Charles Lord telephoned me to engage my

services as a bankruptcy lawyer. I had no prior connection with Lord and assume Lord simply found my office number in the yellow pages. At our initial meeting it was obvious Charles Lord was deeply in debt and needed to file for protection under the bankruptcy laws. He gave me the impression he had not discussed his situation with anybody else before coming to me.

The Domino Effect

Fullen filed Lord's bankruptcy petition on July 1, 1993. The facade Lord had so carefully built up, was about to crumble. Triggered by the Knox brothers' adventure in June, the FBI began investigating Lord's background. Jo Anne Overall learned that, when Charles Lord retired from the Defense Depot as its chief financial officer, he was highly regarded and respected. At the request of the military commanding officer at the Depot, the Shelby County Mayor even declared a "Charles Lord Day" at Lord's retirement party.

When the FBI began peeling away those layers of regard, they found something thoroughly rotten underneath. Through the years, Lord had often spoken of his earth moving business to his co-workers. He had taken out loans from the Credit Union using Caterpillar bulldozers as collateral. At the time he retired, these loan balances amounted to over $400,000. A check by the FBI of the serial numbers with Caterpillar in Peoria, Illinois, proved the numbers to be fictitious and fraudulent.

Lord now appeared to be guilty of a Federal crime by obtaining the loans using false information. There was more information to come from the Federal Defense Depot.

The FBI Contacts Mike and Mary Coward

Mike and his wife Mary took a trip to Nashville,

Tennessee, in July. They had originally asked Charles and Sylvia to join them, but the Lords had declined. The week they returned Mike received a frightening call from Jo Anne Overall. Rumors were beginning to fly about Charles, but he couldn't believe them.

Jo Anne cautioned Mike to stay away from the church. She warned him not to have anything to do with anybody at the church. She further advised him that, if he did otherwise, he and his family might be in danger.

When he asked her if it had anything to do with Charles Lord, she said she could not say, but cautioned him once more against having anything to do with the church.

The Cowards stayed away from the church a couple of weeks, then resumed attending. Mike does not recall speaking with Charles or Sylvia Lord again. His wife recalls seeing Sylvia Lord at the Kroger store after that, but they did not talk.

Friends and Neighbors

Jo Anne also called Malinda Lancaster and told her they were bringing Charles in for a polygraph test. She asked Malinda not to talk to the Lords or anyone else about this.

One evening, in tears Sylvia Lord went to another neighbor, who asked to remain anonymous. Going through the mail, she had opened an official document that said Charles had filed for bankruptcy. Sylvia was completely shocked and distraught. Charles had always handled all the finances and Sylvia said she had no idea there were such debts.

Tommy Fullen, the bankruptcy attorney for Charles, says he seemed perfectly normal, just like any of his other bankruptcy clients. But soon Tommy Fullen and the rest of the world would learn there was nothing normal about this case.

CHAPTER FIFTEEN

From *The Commercial Appeal*, August 7, 1993:

ROBERTS RIDDLE YEAR OLD, UNSOLVED ODD CALLS FEED TORMENT OF SEARCH

Source: Chris Conley

Whenever the mystery of Martha 'Doe' Roberts's disappearance fades from the minds of her friends and family, a voice on the telephone brings it back. "The case goes along for a while, then all of a sudden things pop up," said Malinda Lancaster, one of Roberts's best friends, who received one of the baffling calls last December.

It was a year ago today that Roberts, 65, vanished from the 150-acre Eads home she shared with her husband, Allen.

The FBI has followed leads, digging up a small dump on the couple's property, questioning friends, relatives, former employees. A grand jury has convened to hear evidence in the case. Still the mystery continues.

In the past year, a man has made dozens of calls to friends, claiming to know what happened to Roberts and demanding money. The most recent call was logged in June.

The day his wife disappeared, Allen Roberts reported receiving a ransom call from a man who demanded $100,000 but didn't say where to leave the money. Roberts said he received another call in October.

In some of the phone calls, the caller suggests Roberts hired someone to kidnap his wife but had reneged on the deal.

"That is totally untrue and I resent it" Roberts said. "(The caller) is trying to blacken my name. I am growing weary of the crap."

FBI officials said this week they know who the caller is and are hoping to use that information to discover what happened to Mrs. Roberts. Agent in charge Robert Wright said the FBI is committed to solving the "probable homicide" of Mrs. Roberts.

Another close friend, Brenda Williamson, said she saw Mrs. Roberts last Aug. 3.

"She mentioned fears she had of people, not serious, some business things," Williamson said.

"I still look in ditches, I keep looking for her," she said.

The caller told William Paul Knox of Southaven, a nephew of the Roberts couple, to bring $85,000 to a certain location and await instructions. Knox said the caller did not appear.

Knox, like other family members, believes Mrs. Roberts was kidnapped and died shortly after, possibly in an asthma attack. He, like others, resents the caller's implications that Allen Roberts is responsible for his wife's disappearance.

"I told the FBI they were off base in suspecting him," said Patsy Dunn, a niece of the Roberts couple.

Dunn also said she did not believe Doe Roberts would leave on her own.

"She would not leave my mother suffering. She would not leave her family hurting." Dunn's mother, Jewell, is Doe Roberts's sister.

Allen Roberts and Martha Eudora Jones were married in 1948, in Olive Branch, Miss. She worked at the old Rogers Cafeteria downtown; he installed insulation and weather stripping.

In the 1950s, they bought the Magnolia Grill on Union, but in 1961 they left the restaurant business and started Holiday Auto Parts, which expanded to six stores.

Friends and family members described the Roberts couple as generous benefactors. They did not have children, but they showered attention on nieces and nephews. Dunn said Allen Roberts was hurt when she turned down his offer to put her child through school.

Last Aug. 7, Allen Roberts reported his wife missing after he said a caller threatened to kill her and demanded $100,000. The caller hung up without further instructions.

The day before, Roberts said that a man identifying himself as Sam Wagner from Indiana made an Aug. 7 appointment with Roberts to see a Fayette County subdivision Roberts was developing.

Roberts now believes the call was made to draw him out of the house.

He said the first ransom call came that evening. Roberts said he also got a call in October from a man with a foreign accent. The call was traced to a pay phone in Bartlett, he said.

Roberts said he was upset that many other people contacted went to the FBI, and he was kept in the dark. "They were told to keep quiet," he said. "I felt a deep resentment."

Roberts said he has taken two polygraph tests and passed. The FBI has not commented on the polygraphs.

"They asked me did I kill my wife. . ." he said. "It was a direct question. The answer I gave was a negative answer, a truthful answer."

Roberts said the FBI searched his house with his consent two months, after his wife's disappearance.

"I didn't have anything to hide, anything to lose," said Roberts who says he has not been subpoenaed to the grand jury.

Those who know Mrs. Roberts say they are continually reminded of her absence. Members of the Top Spinners square dancing club, who danced with the Roberts at the Eads Civic Club Center, have tried to come to grips with her disappearance.

"We'll miss her; she really loved the community and did a lot for it. It's been devastating, and made people more cautious," said Yvonne Keough, secretary of the club.

Many of them will be there Aug. 11 for a private service for Doe at the United Methodist Church in Eads. Allen Roberts is expected to address the congregation.

"We don't, any of us, know what to think," Lancaster said. "The whole case is real strange. I hope some day it will all come to light."

Hazel Richmond

On Friday, August 20th, I received a call from Jo Anne Overall, asking why the church wrote a check to Charles Lord for $14,000. At first I did not remember and denied having written the check. Then, when given the date Charles deposited the check, October, 26, 1992, it came back to me.

Charles had told me he was searching for a better interest rate for the church's Certificates of Deposit. He said that if we consolidated the CD's into one, we would get a better return on our money. He telephoned me to say his own Credit Union had the best rate and he was going to move the CD's there.

I told Jo Anne I remembered that, later Charles met with the church Finance Committee and said he'd added $14,000 from his own account in order meet a minimum deposit amount for the best rate. Charles brought a copy of the check he wrote and I reimbursed him from the church's checking account. This was the check in question.

Jo Anne told me that I should bring all the church's financial records to the Federal Building and meet with them the following Monday. I got busy immediately and began calling the banks and getting all the current balances on the accounts.

After the call to the first bank, my hands began to tremble. Each subsequent call brought the same unbelievable news. The Scholarship Fund, the Building Fund, the Certificates of Deposit, all were gone—cleaned out.

I called Mike Coward and asked him to set up a special meeting of the Finance Committee. I met with Lloyd Hight, Joe Clem, and Mike.

Further Contact Between the FBI and Mike Coward

Hazel's news came as a shock to Mike. The church had its money invested in CDs ever since the year that he had been Chairman of the Board of Stewards. To his knowledge they had been safe and secure and he had not heard anything further about these funds until then.

Jo Anne called him on Sunday evening, August 22nd and told him Charles had embezzled the church's money and would be arrested soon. Mike found it incredible that Charles had taken the money.

Hazel Richmond

Monday morning I worked hard to gather and organize the church's records. I packed the material in a box and arrived in downtown Memphis a little before one o'clock that afternoon. I had several more surprises in store that day.

My visits to downtown Memphis were infrequent, and I had a hard time finding a place to park. The Federal Building in downtown Memphis faces Front Street and the Mississippi River on the west. The eastern side faces the Mid-America Mall and is part of a complex of government buildings.

After several minutes of driving around, I parked some distance away and remember how I struggled to carry the heavy box of records in the August heat. As I was walking up the outside steps to the Federal Building, I heard someone call my name.

"Hazel!"

I looked around and was surprised to see Brother Jim DeBardeleban. He walked up and told me that he, too, had been called to come. He took the box from me and we went to the front of the Federal Building, but couldn't find a way to get in. We walked around to the north side, but again found no entrance.

As we went from door to door, lugging the boxes in the heat, I told the pastor, "Charles Lord has cleaned us out." He made no immediate response. His face was as blank as a mask.

We finally found the main entrance and rode the elevator up in silence. Just a few moments later, when Brother Jim and I entered a small waiting area, we found Charles and Sylvia Lord sitting there. Both of us went suddenly pale and began sweating. Brother Jim never spoke a word during our encounter with the Lords.

After a few moments, Charles came over and took my hand, pleading for my forgiveness. His voice trembled as he said, "I'm sorry I took the money, but I didn't do that *other thing*."

At that moment, I had no idea what "other thing" Charles was talking about. I told Charles, "I'll work on it."

Sylvia sat whimpering about no one giving her any support. I took this to mean that Sylvia was referring to Brother Jim's lack of pastoral care.

I felt unusually bold that day, and got up, went over to Sylvia, and said, "You know how you're always blaming others when things go wrong? Well, you better do some thinking."

After a few minutes, the Lords left and Reverend DeBardeleban and I went in for our meeting. I was angry when I went in and told the agents, "I regard the presence of the Lords as an insult!"

Present at this meeting, in addition to Jo Anne Overall, were a male FBI agent whose name I don't recall, Shelby County Attorney General John Pierotti, and a male associate from his office. All of them offered their apologies. They explained that the presence of the Lords had been accidental. Despite this, I was left with the impression that this might have been planned.

Some weeks later, I learned that Charles and Sylvia were there to meet with the FBI to prove that Sylvia had not participated in the kidnapping and murder of Doe.

At the meeting, I gave the FBI and District Attorney a written summary of what I had found, but they did not take any of the records I brought. DeBardeleban, his face grim and white, remained silent, while I did all the talking. I have no memory of there being any discussion as to whether the church would press charges against Lord. I also cannot remember exactly when or how Lord got the authority to move the CD's and/or clear the church's accounts. As Chair of Finance, Lord had managed to gain access to these over time.

On Wednesday evening Charles was arrested for the abduction and murder of Doe Roberts. The news spread across the Eads community like wildfire.

The next step would be to locate Doe's body.

Jewel Knox

When I received word that Charles Lord had confessed to kidnapping and murdering Doe, I joined my son, William Paul, on Thursday afternoon at the location where Doe's body was supposed to be. I was on the river bank, while the dive team searched for Doe's body, but I was convinced that Doe wasn't in the river.

I came to Memphis 'cause I just knew that today was the day they were going to find Doe. I was standing there on the Wolf River's bank when Rudy Davis came up. I think he was directing the divers. He had been a friend of Doe's and Allen's.

While we stood there watching the divers work, I told him, "You're going to find Doe today, but it's not going to be in the river."

Later Ramona came over to us and William Paul reminded her of their bet: a steak dinner if Charles Lord was guilty and Allen was innocent. Ramona came back with a quick quip that the case wasn't closed yet.

Mark McDaniel

Upon Tommy Fullen's recommendation, Sylvia Lord retained me to represent her husband Charles. Once Charles learned he had replaced Allen Roberts as the prime suspect and that the FBI had built a compelling case against him, he knew he needed a criminal defense attorney.

To avoid the State from seeking the death penalty, the Attorney General insisted Lord would have to confess to the crime and lead the authorities to Doe's body.

After the search on the river had been going on for a couple of days, Ramona called me and said, "Please ask Charles if Doe's really out here. I've got a lot of people out here and I'm afraid that someone's going to get hurt."

I went to the Shelby County Jail and spoke with Lord, who finally told me where he really had buried Doe, but wouldn't give me permission to tell Ramona and Jo Anne until I had a personal conference with the Attorney General to confirm the terms of our plea bargain. I called Ramona back and told her, "Tell your people to take a coffee break."

* * *

From *The Commercial Appeal*, August 27, 1993:

FAYETTE NEIGHBOR IS ARRESTED IN DOE ROBERTS KIDNAP, DEATH

*Source: Chris Conley and Rob Johnson.
Staff reporters Lisa Jennings, Lawrence Buser and
Quintin Robinson contributed to this story.*

Authorities today expect to charge a Fayette County man with a record of financial problems in the kidnapping and death of Martha "Doe" Roberts who disappeared from her Eads home last August. Charles J. Lord, who is an acquaintance of the Roberts family, was arrested Wednesday night by Shelby County Sheriff's deputies and FBI agents.

He is being held in the Shelby County Jail, where he has been on suicide watch as a precaution, according to sheriff's officials. Lord faces possible charges of murder, especially aggravated kidnapping and extortion, according to his attorney Mark McDaniel.

Lord, 59, a former comptroller at the Memphis Defense Distribution Depot, recently filed for bankruptcy. And authorities are looking into missing money from Eads United Methodist Church—where Lord and the 65-year-old Roberts were members—and a large loan that Lord received from the defense depot credit union.

"We do have a confession," Shelby County Sheriff A. C. Gilless said. "And we have every reason to believe she's dead."

Authorities will resume the search today for Roberts's body in the Wolf River, about two miles north of Piperton in Fayette County. Thursday, a dive team combed the river beneath the Alec Spiller Bridge on Chulahoma about a mile north of Tenn. 57. The search began about 1:30 p.m. and was suspended about 4:30 when a thunderstorm moved into the area.

Gilless said authorities went with Lord to the site Wednesday night where he told them he dumped Roberts's body over the bridge.

Roberts disappeared Aug. 7, 1992 from the 150-acre Eads home she shared with her husband, Allen Roberts. Sheriff's officials said Thursday they believe Lord tricked Roberts into getting into his car by saying that her husband had been in an accident. Officials also believe Lord killed the woman the same day he abducted her and then dumped her body into the Wolf River.

Soon after the disappearance, the woman's husband made a plea for his wife's release. She had a life-threatening asthmatic condition that required daily medication. The medicine was left behind, her husband said.

Thursday, Lord's attorney said that "medication had nothing to do with" Roberts's death. McDaniel said he could not comment on what Lord told authorities.

"He's (Lord) cooperated completely," McDaniel said. "We just want to bring the matter to a head."

142

Allen Roberts said Thursday he hoped the arrest would bring the issue to a close.

"I might get an opportunity to feel real anger at someone," he said. "I feel I really need to get mad. . . I'd like to think it's over now. If the good Lord's willing, it'll be over. I'd like very much to bring it to an end and put it behind me."

Authorities would not comment on many aspects of the case. Gilless would not say if Allen Roberts is a suspect.

"The case is still under investigation. . . we do not know where it will lead us," he said. He would not discuss possible motives.

But authorities said Thursday they were looking into an approximate $300,000 loan Lord obtained from the defense depot credit union, and also the disappearance of roughly $86,000 from the church, where Lord was a financial officer.

The loan was reflected in a Chapter 7 bankruptcy petition Lord filed last month in U.S. Bankruptcy Court. The petition listed $373,106 in total liabilities and $128,300 in assets.

A break in the case came three weeks ago when FBI officials announced that they knew who had made a series of ransom demands in the past year to friends and relatives of the Roberts. They would not identify the caller. Thursday, Gilless said the caller was Lord, who is married and has three children.

Two weeks ago, divers dragged three ponds for Roberts's body. One of the ponds was near Lord's property.

Allen Roberts reported receiving a ransom call the evening his wife disappeared. He said he received a second ransom call in October from a man with a foreign accent. Roberts said the caller never told him where to bring the $100,000 ransom.

Roberts said after the first ransom call, he was told to smash the answering machine on the driveway.

Roberts also said he had received a call from a man identifying himself as "Sam Wagner" the night before his wife's disappearance.

The man asked to see a home Roberts was developing in Fayette County.

Roberts said he believed the call was designed to draw him out of the house.

A friend of Doe Roberts, Brenda Williamson, said she went through the Roberts home right after the disappearance in an effort to help solve the mystery. Doe Roberts was wearing a pantsuit and black shoes, as though on her way to a business meeting.

Doe Roberts had recently had cataract surgery, so she was unable to drive herself.

Williamson speculated that Doe Roberts was with someone she knew that day.

Lord's neighbors expressed shock following the arrest. "It's hard to believe it could be true," said neighbor Ray Schauboreck. "He seemed like a good guy. . . He was active in the church."

Lon Lancaster said, "There wasn't any suspicion at all, until lately, when authorities dragged ponds in the area.

He said he and his wife had been to dinner at the Lords' residence lately and the subject had come up.

Lord, he said, did not seem overly concerned.

"I'm glad they're making what I hope is some possible progress," said Bill Simmons, Allen Roberts's nephew.

"It'll never really be over, but if they find her remains we can bury her and get on with life. You need to bury your loved ones."

Simmons said Roberts plans to move from his Eads home, where too much reminds him of his missing wife.

Roberts would not say where he was thinking of moving in order to protect his privacy.

Friends, Neighbors, and Deputies

Malinda Lancaster and other neighbors on Great Oaks were shocked and disturbed when Friday evening, about dark, deputies came and blocked off the Lords' house. They put up barricades, just where the road curves. She walked down to ask the officers what was going on. The man told her, "Listen to the news in the morning."

By nine o'clock the daylight was gone. In the Lords' backyard the Sheriff's deputies, and others held flashlights that cast long shadows into the surrounding trees. Dr. Berryman and his helper slowly, patiently removed cement pieces and soil with hand trowels. Then suddenly a delicate length of bone became exposed. The search was over. Doe Roberts lay before them, where she had waited through the long, long year.

At that moment, no one, not even her family and loved ones, could hold her more precious than those who stood over her.

Lieutenant Goodwin of Forensics says their motto is, "'We work for God and we didn't kill 'em.' We're evidence men. Maybe the FBI can find killers in their computers, but we love physical evidence."

Goodwin and "Tank" Scallion had been searching for Doe's body on the river banks all day. They hadn't been home yet, but they decided to stand watch through the night.

Detective Kelly ordered a deputy to watch in a patrol car in the front of the Lords' driveway. A funeral canopy was set over the grave. The detectives pulled together some lawn chairs for their vigil throughout that sultry, mosquito-infested August night. As the hours stretched on, they talked about another case—searching, probing their memories for any connection to Lord—trying to link him to Teresa Butler, a young woman who had disappeared in the same area in 1986.

Early in the morning Goodwin's wife brought the men fresh clothes. Goodwin and Tank rinsed off the night's sweat under the garden hose. They had another long day ahead.

Malinda Lancaster tried to reach the Lords' backyard several times the next day, but couldn't get past the deputies. So she went to the Adams, who lived on Wildwood, but whose lot bordered on the back of the Lord property. Determined, she would eventually win access to the site she so desired.

Berryman and Sims returned with their trowels before eight the next morning. Jo Anne and other FBI agents, along with Inspector Ramona Swain, arrived about the same time as Mark McDaniel. They all took their positions over the grave. Berryman carefully, painstakingly chipped at the concrete encasing the body. By mid-morning they were able to lift it off and Doe lay before them, whole and remarkably well preserved.

Apparently Lord had thought that by using regular lime he would hasten decomposition of Doe's body. Had he used quicklime, he would have succeeded. That was how the Revolutionaries in France had summarily disposed of their enemies' bodies that were guillotined during the Reign of Terror. Quicklime is still used by farmers and health officials for disposing of dead animals. But regular lime produced exactly the opposite effect—her appearance was like that of an ancient Egyptian queen who had been artfully preserved. The gray, shrunken face was readily recognizable by the high cheekbones and the curve of her chin.

During the morning Fayette County deputies held the neighbors at bay, but during the afternoon Malinda Lancaster found a place in the neighbor's yard less than 100 feet away. When they lifted the cement cap, Malinda was almost overcome by the sudden release of a sickeningly sweet smell.

She said, "I had never seen a body before, but I was bound and determined to find out what was going on."

Mark McDaniel, who was standing over the grave, said, "That smell stayed in my clothes all day."

Kelly and Goodwin do not remember any odor at all.

Berryman and his staff lifted the body with great tenderness and care. They carried it to a special van parked in the driveway. They drove straight to the Memphis Forensic center at the University of Tennessee Medical School in downtown Memphis and immediately performed an autopsy.

The Autopsy

As difficult as it may have been for Allen and for the rest of Doe's family, there was a story to be told Doe had waited that long year to tell. Doe could speak only through her body, so those performing the autopsy had to serve as her translators. Together the detectives and the pathologists worked to understand, to hear the tale the flesh wanted to tell.

The Memphis Forensic Center did not yet have the perfect tool. They used blood type testing and toxicology screens, and their eyes, but the tale was mostly told through deduction. In 1993, DNA testing was still on the horizon. There were no wounds, no signs of violent death, so they accepted Lord's admission of suffocation as the cause of death. The toxicology screens of the liver failed to show the presence of any drugs. Time had done its work, but so had Lt. Goodwin.

As Goodwin and McDaniel stood over the body that morning, he said to McDaniel, "That body is in such good condition, we'll be able to discover a lot.

"For example," Goodwin told Lord's lawyer, "any drugs used may come out in the autopsy." He paused as Mark McDaniel looked closely at the body again, then continued, "Well, you know, we'll probably find evidence of any sexual activity, too."

That was a tactic Goodwin had used before. He knew criminals often confess to what they think the detectives know.

From her dental records, a positive identification confirmed the body was that of Doe Roberts.

Ann Richmond

We do not have televisions in our work areas, but I heard there was going to be an announcement. So I went to a TV and turned it on so I could see the noon newscast.

I couldn't believe it.

Friends, Relatives, and Neighbors

The Sunday after Charles Lord's arrest, the media besieged Eads United Methodist once more. Newspaper people sat with the members of the congregation, taking pictures. The TV cameras were everywhere, filming the church and the congregation inside.

Allen had begun seeing me every evening. We knew, if Doe came back, he would have to go back with her. My situation was awkward, but I accepted it. I never wished anything but the best for Doe, even if it meant my losing Allen. After all, she had been his loving wife for over forty years, so, if she should return, Allen's place would be with her.

It did me a world of good, though, to be with Allen. As we saw more and more of each other, he seemed to be returning to what must have been his former self. He began kidding with me and making jokes when we'd go out to dinner. He'd notice funny things about other people and tell me, like when a woman left her purse open and it was about to spill over, or when a man of obvious Italian extraction was talking at a nearby table and kept waving his arms for emphasis. I'd try not to laugh and embarrass us.

We went dancing three or four nights a week. Being used to going to bed at 9:30 and rising early for work, I found myself exhausted. I told Allen I couldn't keep up with him. He went by himself to other clubs, where he would dance with more experienced dancers, but he always went alone. When he wanted company he always came back to me.

After we started going out regularly, I learned people had begun gossiping about us. Friends and clients confided in me during moments when we were alone in my salon that there were rumors Allen had done Doe in so he could start seeing me. Some even had said I was Allen's accomplice. You can't fight vicious gossip. All you can do is pretend to ignore it, and act like you are. People might say, "Don't let it get to you," but how can you help that? You see folks day in and day out and think they are your friends. Then you hear what they say behind your back!

What makes people say such cruel and thoughtless things? The worst ones seemed to be from the Methodist

Church in Eads, the same church Doe and Allen had generously supported for so many years. It seemed that two or three women who had been Doe's friends now were targeting me and trying to turn Allen's friends against him because of me. The pastor might have made a difference if he had stepped in on Allen's behalf, but it appeared he might even have believed Allen was guilty.

It didn't seem to do Allen any good to go back to that church, anyway. He acted like he enjoyed attending Bellevue Baptist with me, and we started going there together regularly.

Although Allen's emotional health appeared to be improving, he was still a much shaken man. This was brought home to me whenever we found ourselves in places he and Doe had frequented and he would suddenly start to cry. All I could do would be to take his hand and gently squeeze it, or if nobody was around, give him a hug and hold him until his crying spell passed.

He confided to me that the detectives had told him so much time had already passed that the chances of finding his wife alive now were slim to none. That realization didn't help his spirits any.

The more we saw of each other, the more I realized how attached I was becoming to Allen. Like my late husband Louis, Allen was a quiet man who sometimes, actually most of the time, had a hard time expressing his feelings. Keeping them bottled up inside might have caused him to have a stroke or heart attack. Or, like Louis, it might have driven him to suicide.

Instead, he found an outlet talking with me. And talk he did, sometimes for hours. He was a good talker, and he could talk about almost anything. He had traveled a lot around our country. He had a pilot's license and had even flown his own airplane. He'd scuba dived and done some deep sea fishing. Doe and Allen had struggled together and built a very successful business, then spread out into home building and other investments. When they were finally starting to enjoy the American Dream, it was taken from them by Doe's abduction.

Now, for whatever it meant, I found myself more and more standing in her place. Allen had become a very important part of my life, and I the same for him. As 1993 passed from winter to spring, he began hinting that he wanted me to give up my business so we could spend more time together.

"Allen," I said, "I can't just walk away from my customers. Many of them are my friends, too. I've been doing hair for some of them for over 28 years!" That usually ended the discussion. But it didn't stop Allen from bringing it up again.

One Sunday afternoon when the spring weather had turned warm enough, Pat and her husband Larry invited Allen and me over for a cookout. Larry was great with steaks and had some prime beef ready to grill for all of us.

As we sat on their beautiful patio dining on our steaks, Allen looked across at the vacant lot next door. There was a For Sale sign on it

Out of the blue he said, "Esther, I think we should buy this lot and build a house."

His remark puzzled me. Was he talking about an investment? I knew he built and sold homes in his business. If that was what he meant, I didn't like the idea of him mixing his business with my family's property. But he did not sound like that was what he intended.

No, instead, he was talking about us. He had said "we."

Up to that time, Allen had never expressed his feelings toward me. I'd never heard him say how he felt, certainly not use words like "love" or "marriage." Despite his loving companionship, I knew that marriage was not an option as long as there was any hope of Doe's return. Yet I realized he was talking about a commitment, so solidly shown by his willingness to buy this land next to my daughter's home and build a house for us!

True to his word, Allen bought that lot. He made me sign the papers putting the property in only my name, saying, "If Doe comes back, you'll still have a home next door to your daughter and her family. I want you to be taken care of."

In July, a crew came in and laid the foundation. Allen let me help with the plans and the design. His eyes would sparkle when he'd ask, "Hon, what do you think about the garage?" Or, "Is the patio large enough?" Workmen began framing and, before we knew it, our new home had been built.

When the construction crew began installing the inside walls, Allen handed me his credit card. With a twinkle in his eyes, he said, "Hon, you're in charge of the interior decorating. You'll need this for. . . wallpaper, carpet, and appliances."

He studied my face as he slowly finished speaking. Obviously noticing my smile growing bigger and wider with each word, his face also broke into a broad grin.

I had no idea how much work was involved in selecting those materials. Having budgeted myself all my life, I still searched for bargains and materials on sale. There are lots of stores in the Memphis area and many run ads regularly in the daily newspaper. I checked each day to see if anything we wanted and needed was on sale. Each time I made a new purchase I'd proudly tell Allen how I found a good deal and spent his money wisely. That always brought a smile to his face. It made me feel so good to see him smile.

In August of 1993, when Allen and I had returned to my condominium in Memphis after an evening of square dancing, he received the phone call we had long awaited and dreaded. Allen told me, "That was Ramona Swain. She's told me to meet her and Jo Anne at my house. Will you come with me?"

When we arrived at his home on George R. James Road, Jo Anne and Ramona were already there, waiting in Jo Anne's car. Seeing us, they got out and accompanied us inside. Sitting in the den, Jo Anne broke the news, "Mr. Roberts, we have located Doe's body."

She went on to say that Charles Lord had confessed to Doe's abduction and murder and that he was under arrest. His attorney had worked a deal where Lord's confession would spare him from the District Attorney seeking the death penalty. She told Allen, "This means you are no longer a suspect. I'm sorry if we caused you any trouble."

That was the closest thing to an apology Allen ever received from the authorities, but we thought it was decent of Jo Anne to try. Ramona, on the other hand, remained aloof and continued to act as though she still doubted Allen's innocence.

Allen always tried to contain his emotions, but when he heard the news both his anger at Lord and his grief for Doe were so plainly visible. Once the detectives left, I held him close as he broke down and wept.

CHAPTER SIXTEEN

"He was a man of lies. He just couldn't do anything else."

Allen Roberts, 1996

The Confessions of Charles Lord

Perhaps the only smart thing Charles Lord did after his criminal schemes began to unravel was follow his bankruptcy attorney Tommy Fullen's advice to hire Mark McDaniel for his criminal defense counsel.

Mark is highly regarded among members of the Memphis Bar Association as one of the most capable in his field, and his representation of Charles Lord is a testament to his reputation. Having admitted criminal activity to the FBI, Lord sought McDaniel's professional services to mitigate what had to be severe punishment when his guilt was determined. Tennessee was one of the first states to reinstate the death penalty after the U. S. Supreme Court ruled under what guidelines it met the tests of Constitutionality. If prosecuted to a conviction, it would be certain that Lord would be sentenced to death.

Another salient consideration was the level of culpability that Sylvia Lord shared with her husband. This applied to both Doe's abduction and murder, and the financial crimes of fraud and embezzlement Charles had committed.

Statistically, it would be impossible to try every criminal case. Most defendants lack resources to hire their own attorney and, under the famous case of *Miranda v. California,* the State is required to provide them with a public defender. Even the State, with seemingly limitless resources, however, cannot afford to spend the time and money to prosecute every case.

In order to keep the system operating, the prosecutor and the defense attorney commonly enter into an agreement for the defendant known as a "plea bargain." In exchange for obtaining a guilty plea from the defendant the prosecutor agrees to ask the court to impose a more lenient sentence than the defendant would receive if tried and convicted.

Using his knowledge, experience, and expertise, Mark McDaniel struck a plea bargain with the Fayette County Attorney General that, in exchange for Charles Lord's confession as to the abduction and death of Doe Roberts, they would not seek the death penalty, but instead a life sentence. Two additional stipulations entered into between McDaniel on Lord's behalf and the prosecutors were that there would be no investigation of Sylvia Lord and that she would also not be sought to be held accountable for any of the monies her husband had illegally obtained. What McDaniel and the authorities did not anticipate was the wild deviations Lord would present in three different confessions he gave.

The first two were so disparate that the prosecutor told McDaniel if Charles did not tell the truth once and for all, the plea bargain would be withdrawn. His third confession was the one presented to Judge Jon Kerry Blackwood and accepted as authentic.

What had previously only been speculated about was now fact. The murder had been committed in Fayette County. Sheriff Kelly had great respect for R.T. Goodwin's skills as an interrogator and requested that Goodwin do the interrogation on the behalf of Fayette County. Kelly and Goodwin left the autopsy and immediately drove the few blocks that separate the Forensic Center at the University of Tennessee from the Criminal Justice Building in the heart of downtown Memphis.

At 2:45 p.m. the small group gathered in the Shelby County Sheriff's Department conference room on ninth floor. Around the table were Lt. Goodwin and Chief Ray Mills of Shelby County, Sheriff Kelly and Captain Bobby Riles of Fayette County, Mark McDaniel and Charles Lord.

Notable by their absence were the chief investigators, Jo Anne Overall and Ramona Swain. The women were not informed about the session. Some interdepartmental politics may have been at work here, but no one will speculate about their absence at this point.

The following contains pertinent excerpts from the official Confession transcript. Where glaring disparities appear or pertinent facts are stated by Lord, and sometimes for sake of propriety, editorial comments have been made in italics.

Goodwin began by asking Lord about the previous confession on August 26th:

GOODWIN: Could you briefly go over the contents of that statement?

LORD: Well, the statement talks about how I kidnapped and caused the death of, ah, Martha Doe Roberts. It also contains some outright lies as to an affair between Mrs. Roberts and myself. Ah, there are a number of other untruths in the statement and I desire now to tell the truth and, and get on with it. There was another statement earlier that was, ah, also not true.

[There followed several questions regarding the false statements Lord made in the first two typed confessions. Then Goodwin picked up the questioning about the chronology of the kidnapping.]

GOODWIN:. . . but it is true. . . that you called the residence prior to going over there in reference to a real estate deal?

LORD: Yes

GOODWIN: To try and make sure that ah. . .

LORD: Mr. Roberts was not there. . .

GOODWIN: Mr. Roberts was not at home?

LORD: That's true.

GOODWIN: And that part of both the statements are [sic] true?

LORD: Yes.

GOODWIN: Okay, do you, off the top of your head, do you remember in both the previous statements you made, how you approached the residence and how you got in the residence? Can you recall what you told Insp. Swain and The FBI Agent how you encountered Mrs. Roberts for the first time, in the two previous statements?

LORD: I think in the first statement I said. . . I drove up and Doe came around the side of the house. She had been to the orchard or something and she was wearing a, a smock and maybe slippers. And the next time I believe I said she came to the door.

GOODWIN: You knocked on the door and she came to the door?

LORD: Yeah.

GOODWIN: Okay. Both those, those, are contradictory, is that not correct?

LORD: That's correct.

GOODWIN: Okay. All right, in the new statement that we're taking today, what was your contact with her at her house and how did you manage to get her outside the house?

LORD: I told her that her husband had been in an accident over at this subdivision and she needed to come with me real quick. She said, ah, "Well is he hurt bad? How bad is it?" and I said, "Just come and go with me" and she, ah, she grabbed her purse and, ah, came out the door and got in the truck.

GOODWIN: Okay that's that statement that you just made, in both the previous statements did you not relate that, well, your first statement you used the ruse that he had been involved in an accident to get her out of the house, is that not true?

LORD: That's true.

[Goodwin took some time to make Lord distinguish lies from supposed truth in the first and second statements. Then the detective probed into just how long Lord had been planning the crime.]

GOODWIN: Did you ever make the statement on or off the record to the FBI or the Sheriff's Department that you had been planning this as far back as May or July?

LORD: I don't believe I did.

GOODWIN: Okay you don't remember that?

LORD: No sir, I don't.

GOODWIN: But it's possible since it occurred on August 7th, is that the date that you remember that it, that this occurred on?

LORD: Yes, yes.

GOODWIN: So it would be possible that it could have been sometime in July?

LORD: Yes sir it could be.

GOODWIN: Okay that you planned this?

LORD: Yes.

GOODWIN: Okay and in the, okay, we'll, let's stay with that then, ah, when she came to the door, what was she wearing?

LORD: She was wearing a blue blouse of—I guess that's a blouse, of some sort and I believe a, ah, a checkered skirt and blue shoes.

GOODWIN: Okay, this description of this, ah, these clothes does not match either statement that you made before?

LORD: That's correct.

GOODWIN: In both those statements you said that she was wearing a brownish, a brown moo-moo?

LORD: And that's, those were false statements.

GOODWIN: Okay. All right, can you tell me what difference it would make in the first, second statement and the one that you're giving now as to what she was wearing?

LORD: Well, this time I'm telling the truth.

GOODWIN: I know, but I understand that. I'm not questioning that. What I'm saying is what in your first statements did, was it important to say, that it was a brownish moo-moo?

LORD: I really don't know. I can't answer that. I just made it up.

GOODWIN: Okay. She's at the door, blue blouse, checkered skirt, she's grabbed her purse, she's got in the car, did, was there, did she go back in the house for medicine?

LORD: No, she did not.

GOODWIN: Okay, and, at one point in time either on the record or in the statement you stated that she had went in and got some medicine, is that true?

LORD: That's true.

GOODWIN: Okay and in that same statement that we mentioned that she went in and got the medicine, that was the contradictory about the purse stating in the first statement it was clearly, you clearly remembered a purse around her neck, a purse played into the first statement that you gave the Sheriff's Department. The brown moo-moo clearly played into your first statement with the Sheriff's Department. In the second statement, the clothes are the same but you have no recollection whatsoever of the purse.

LORD: Both of those statements were entirely false.

GOODWIN: Today. . . the clothes have changed. We have a blue blouse and a checkered skirt. We have blue shoes, I think or whatever it was you said, and she's getting in the truck with her purse, and that is a true statement?

LORD: And the purse is, purse is blue, yes.

GOODWIN: Okay. So to stay on this same line of questioning, where are the clothes and where is the purse?

LORD: I burned the clothes in a burning pile that I have on, on the back pond levy. Ah, I clipped the buttons off and I believe I also, ah, cut off the, ah, metal fasteners on the purse—I took everything out of the purse that would not burn. I remember there was a pill box and maybe a lipstick—things like that. Ah, I put those things in my pocket and later I disposed of them along, ah, Seward Road between the house and, uptown Seward, uptown Eads. The rest was, ah, was burned in the burning pile I mentioned.

GOODWIN: Okay, what about keys?

LORD: Keys?

GOODWIN: Uh-huh

LORD: Ah, she had some keys and I also disposed of those keys. I believe I, I believe they were on a ring and I believe I threw those out one at a time.

GOODWIN: Okay.

LORD: They are all on—scattered along the south side of, ah, Seward Road. At that time of year the weeds were, were pretty high, and as I would drive along, I would throw them out one at a time.

GOODWIN: Okay when was this that this was done in reference to first arrival—her house and her getting in the truck?

LORD: Are you talking about. . .

GOODWIN: When you threw the stuff out the window of the truck?

LORD: Oh, this was probably Monday or Tuesday of the next week.

GOODWIN: Monday or Tuesday of the next week. Do you remember what day of the week it was that August 7, 1992, occurred on?

LORD: Yes sir. It was on a Friday.

GOODWIN: Okay, so to cover the last two statements, now we've—you in this statement you we've cleared up the purse. Ah, the contents of the purse are on the south side of Seward Road going from your subdivision toward Eads, Tennessee?

LORD: Yes.

GOODWIN: Okay and we've cleared it up about the purse. You're stating that the purse burned in the wood pile on the levy of your pond?

LORD: Yes. I soaked everything, ah, I put everything in a in a plastic garbage bag and soaked it with, ah, with diesel fuel.

GOODWIN: Okay and what day do you recall that it was burned?

LORD: Ah Saturday, Saturday afternoon I believe·

GOODWIN: Okay all right, since that, was anything else there when you burned that stuff?

LORD: Yeah.

GOODWIN: In other words had you been using that as a burn pile?

LORD: Yes, for a number of years.

GOODWIN: Okay.

LORD: Ah, there were a number of limbs and, ah, just yard debris mostly limbs.

GOODWIN: Okay. Can you explain to me why you picked that place? You've got a lot of land there. Ah, that's right on the levy, ah, of your beautiful pond right, right down just a short distance from your gazebo, why would you select that place?

LORD: Well it's behind the levy going down the side of the levy.

GOODWIN: Un-huh.

LORD: And I had been using that to burn brush and stuff ever since we've been there and it was just to me a logical place to burn it.

GOODWIN: Okay

LORD: If my wife saw me out there burning anything, anywhere else, she would probably wonder what I was up to.

GOODWIN: Okay. On the opposite end of the pond toward the compost pile, there were certain logs in a pattern indicating campfire. . .

LORD: Yes. . .

GOODWIN: Type activity, ah, what was the reason for that?

LORD: Well, we originally put that there, ah, when some friends from Utah visited us and we roasted hotdogs and marshmallows out there, that was in September after this, ah, August incident. And then later we had the young people from the church out, out, and, ah, they all roasted weenies and hotdogs and that's just sort of a campfire type thing that hasn't been used but about a year now.

GOODWIN: Okay, can you explain to us why you handled the clothing and the purse in the manner in which you did?

LORD: I was just destroying evidence.

GOODWIN: Okay, can you explain to me why that now we have three, three evidence locations. We've got property from her purse scattered up and down Seward Road. We've got a burn pile that you burned evidence in. We've got a compost pile that we recovered evidence in of the body so we have three locations that we've got evidence recovered. Ah, in a logical way, can you explain why that you didn't think it would all be best kept in one place?

LORD: Well, I, I suppose I thought that if it was all in one place that years from now it would be easier to identify the body. Ah, to throw keys and that kind of thing out along Seward Road as high as the weeds are, ah, nobody ever walks along that road, and then to burn the, ah—I didn't want to throw the purse out because somebody might find or see the purse and the, and the clothes, it was just easier to burn the clothes. If that doesn't make since, I'm sorry, but that's what happened.

[Note that the only time Lord says he's sorry is when he's questioned about the logic of how he destroyed evidence.]

GOODWIN: You didn't believe that the body itself would provide sufficient evidence for an identification?

LORD: No sir.

GOODWIN: Was that your belief at that time?

LORD: My belief was that the lime that I put on the body would destroy everything over a period of time.

GOODWIN: And where did that concept belief come-from?

LORD: Well, years ago I spent some time on a farm with my grandfather and when a farm animal would die, he would dig a pit and pour lime in, I don't really know what for, but ah, he always did so. . .

GOODWIN: What did your grandfather use the concrete for?

LORD: My grandfather never used concrete. I used the concrete because I thought ready-mix had some lime in it and I also thought that if there was a, ah, sort of a hard layer down there, if anybody ever probed, they would think it was a rock and stop digging.

GOODWIN: When you say "probe," what, what are you talking about?

LORD: Ah. . .

GOODWIN: I have a thought that instantly comes to mind when you say, "probe in the ground," I'm just curious of what you mean by "probe."

LORD: Well I didn't know what you people might use or if anybody ever came around you know an x-ray camera or something like this, but later, ah, when the FBI and the Sheriff's Department was out there the second time, some deputy was walking around with some kind of probe that he was sticking in the ground.

GOODWIN: Okay and did they find [anything] the second time they were there?

LORD: Nothing.

GOODWIN: Okay and everything was cool as far as with you at this time you're talking about

LORD: Yeah, oh, yeah, I thought everything was cool.

GOODWIN: And they took the pictures and you thought that, ah, you still hadn't been detected yet?

LORD: Right. That was, that was the time that they sent a diver under the lily pads in the pond and searched the ponds across the street.

GOODWIN: Okay.

LORD: Is that the time you're talking about?

GOODWIN: Yeah, it probably is. That goes back prior to August 26th. . .

LORD: Yeah. I also thought that later if we sold the house and moved what I had, what I had planned to do was to remove—then move the compost pile and maybe build a shed over it or something that would keep it hidden for, for years.

[The following is a rather prosaic discussion concerning whether Lord's house is up for sale. We can only speculate that Goodwin is working to get Lord more relaxed.]

GOODWIN: Is the house for sale now?

LORD: Yes.

GOODWIN: Okay. I noticed there wasn't a sign.

LORD: My wife didn't want a sign up because there's, there's a lot of traffic down there now, ah, you know curiosity seekers riding up and down the road. The other day, for example, she did have a chained a rope across the driveway. Somebody came down there on a 3-wheeler, came off the side of the driveway, tore the yard up, and went around the back and she went out and told them they were

165

trespassing and they left. I think she called the Sheriff's Department.

GOODWIN: Is your, is your house listed in the multiple listings?

LORD: I don't know at this time. My wife is handling that.

GOODWIN: Okay. You don't know whether your wife has an agent?

LORD: She does.

GOODWIN: Okay.

LORD: But I. . . do you remember the name?

McDaniel: All I know is that it was supposed to come out in the paper Sunday.

LORD: Is it, okay?

GOODWIN: I think Sheriff Kelley stated that he recalled that your wife called the Sheriff's Department on the incident that you just related?

LORD: Yeah.

[Now Goodwin returns to the chronology of the kidnapping.]

GOODWIN: Okay. We've, ah, we're in the truck and we're leaving the Roberts' residence in Shelby County, Tennessee and we're en route to where? The next stop of our trip was where?

LORD: The next stop of the trip was, was my house—the garage apartment.

GOODWIN: Okay we've been planning this for a week, maybe two weeks, and. . .

LORD: At least, I'm not sure about it.

GOODWIN: Okay we'll, we'll, we'll go with the two weeks then. We're planning this and for the entire two weeks, you had planned to take Mrs. Roberts to your house?

LORD: To my garage apartment yes.

GOODWIN: Okay and I noticed earlier you stated something that I heard hadn't heard before—that when you told her that her husband had been involved in an accident, in this statement you stated in the subdivision.

LORD: I thought I had said that earlier.

GOODWIN: Okay. For clarity you did tell her that he had had an accident in the subdivision?

LORD: I, I think I did. An accident anyway.

GOODWIN: Okay.

LORD: But see, I knew he had gone to the subdivision so I probably told her in the subdivision.

GOODWIN: Are you talking about the subdivision you live in or. . .

LORD: No I'm talking about the subdivision on Orr Road where Mr. Roberts was building some homes.

GOODWIN: Okay, so if you told her the subdivision, you was talking about where he was building houses?

LORD: Un-huh.

GOODWIN: Okay. So we're en route to your house and how, how long did—would it take you to drive from your house, correction, from her house to your house because I have no idea where her house is.

LORD: Ten minutes

GOODWIN: Okay.

LORD: I guess.

GOODWIN: And how far, during the course of this ten minute drive, is--if she thinks you're going to the subdivision where her husband is located, is she going to know that ya'll are not going there?

LORD: Probably within the first three minutes.

GOODWIN: So three minutes after [you] leave her house, then she's going to know that you're not going to that subdivision if that's what you told her?

LORD: Yes sir that's right.

GOODWIN: Okay at what point during your trip from her house did she become alarmed?

LORD: When you come from her house up George R. James, there are a number of houses and then there is a bridge and there are no houses from there up to ah up Seward Road.

GOODWIN: Un-huh.

LORD: Somewhere between the bridge and Seward Road, I grabbed her by the neck and pulled her down and told her to be quiet, ah, that I was taking her somewhere else, something to this effect. I don't remember the exact words and she said something like, "Well, Charles, what's going on?" and I said, "Well, you must be quiet and don't make another sound." Ah, she might have said "Well, what about Allen?" I told her, "There is nothing wrong with Allen," and I, and I said, "I mean it--you just lay quiet and don't make a sound."

GOODWIN: Okay.

LORD: And I had my hand around her neck at that time.

GOODWIN: Okay. Now just a short [distance] from her house, we're into this thing and there's no going back, is there?

LORD: No sir there's no going back.

GOODWIN: There's no going back. And that's minutes after she came outside of her house with her blue purse and got in your truck and during the whole course of this plan, you were planning on going to your house?

LORD: Yes.

GOODWIN: Okay. What kind of a resistance did she put up?

LORD: She didn't put any resistance up at all. She was very meek. After that, all she would answer me "yes sir" or "no sir."

GOODWIN: Did she sit up in the truck and ride with you or was she leaning down in the truck riding with you?

LORD: No, no, no I had her down. I had her head in my lap and I had my hand around her neck. As I approached the curves to change gears, I would tell her again, "Don't get up. I mean it, stay right where you are." And she said, "Yes, sir."

GOODWIN: Okay. And so we arrived at your house and we're talking ten minutes maybe?

LORD: Approximately yeah.

GOODWIN: Okay and since, there's nothing in either statement in reference to this line of answers that you're giving us so just take it from [where] you've arrived home.

LORD: Okay I got up that that morning. My wife told me that she would probably go to Canada Mall for some shoes. So I thought perhaps that she would leave right behind me. That was the idea that I had.

GOODWIN: Well that for the record, you said Canada Mall, that's at I-40 and Canada Road?

LORD: Right.

GOODWIN: Okay at the Mall there?

LORD: Yes, yes.

[Notice that the only emotion Lord describes during the course of these events is his own fear of getting caught. Not once is there a mention of remorse, except at getting caught.]

LORD: When I got home and pushed the button to raise the garage and I got in, [my wife's] car was there and scared the hell out of me. So I put the door down and sat there for a minute and obviously she didn't see me come in, so then I got Mrs., Roberts out on the on the rider's side and very quickly took her—my garage steps go up to the garage apartment.

GODWIN: Uh-huh.

LORD: And I got in there and passed the door up the steps very quickly, took her into, ah, the bedroom where the air conditioner is, is located, and I had already put a, ah, wooden chair—a high back type chair against the bed. I had strips of rags already ready and I had a belt to go around the chair to keep the chair from tipping over and, ah, I sat her down in the chair. Ah, I put duct tape around her eyes. I don't know why I did that and I tied her securely and told her to stay there, that I was going in the next room and I would be back and if she knew what was good for her, not to make another sound something to that effect.

GOODWIN: But you didn't cover her mouth?

LORD: No I didn't cover her mouth and all she said was, "Yes sir, I won't. . . I won't make any trouble."

GOODWIN: And your wife's car was in the garage when you drove in?

LORD: Yes, yes.

GOODWIN: And what. . . car is [it] that we're talking about?

LORD: My wife's car?

GOODWIN: Un-huh.

LORD: It's an '89 Cadillac Seville.

GOODWIN: Okay and Mrs. Roberts, she, she knows your wife's car?

LORD: Yes.

GOODWIN: Okay and what's the, ah, approximate time that, ah, we've picked her up in your truck from her house?

LORD: About 10:00.

GOODWIN: Approximately 10:00 A.M. in the morning?

LORD: Yeah.

GOODWIN: So around 10:15 A.M., August 11th, 1992, she is. What time was the appointment for you allegedly posing as Sam Wagner to meet her husband at the subdivision on Orr?

LORD: 10:00.

GOODWIN: Okay and that's what you're basing your estimation of the time on?

LORD: Yes. I figured it would take Allen about twenty minutes to get over there and I figured he would keep the appointment on time and ah. . .

GOODWIN: Okay.

LORD: One, one thing I left out. I had a pillow case in the, in the truck. Ah, I believe it was under my seat, and when I just—before I got her out, I put the pillow case over her head and she did say that "I can't breathe." and I said, "Well just don't make any noise and as soon as I as soon as I get you situated, I'll take it off and I'll turn the pillow case later, too.

GOODWIN: And you, ah, so you had to take the pillow case off to put the tape over her eyes?

171

LORD: Yes sir

GOODWIN: And as I recall you said you don't know why you did that and then you put the pillow case back over her head?

LORD: No, I didn't.

GOODWIN: Okay you left it off?

LORD: I left it off.

GOODWIN: Where she could, where [her] mouth was free and you know and she knows your wife is at home?

LORD: I don't believe she saw the car because she was still down.

GOODWIN: Uh-huh

LORD: And I put the pillow case over [and] got her out I don't believe she, I'm not sure if she knew where she was, really·

GOODWIN: Well.

LORD: She could, but I'm not sure.

GOODWIN: Well she had been at your house many times before hadn't she?

LORD: She had been at my house several times, yes. I don't remember her coming in through the garage but remember now, I've got her head down in my lap so all, about all she can see [is], maybe she can see up a little bit, okay, and before I got her out, I did get the pillow case out and put it over her head.

GOODWIN: Un-huh.

LORD: And I don't believe she could see through the pillow case.

GOODWIN: Did you burn the pillow case the same time you burned the ah. . .

LORD: Yes sir, I did.

GOODWIN: Un-huh. So other everything you originally said was okay except you forgot about you put a pillow case over her head so that would explain why she didn't know your wife may be at home. You're not sure whether she knew that or not?

LORD: I'm not sure, no I don't know.

GOODWIN: And she never hollered, she never protested?

LORD: No sir, she never protested at all.

GOODWIN: How, how much money do you think she's worth?

LORD: I didn't know at the time. . .

GOODWIN: Rumor or innuendo or whatever? How much money do you think at that time that she's worth?

LORD: Well I had heard a rumor from a neighbor that they were quote "millionaires."

GOODWIN: And here this lady is—that's a millionaire is in your truck and three minutes later she's realized that something's wrong, you pushed her head down, told her to be quiet, you took her home, raised the garage door, took her inside, pillow case over her head or not, and she's not raising no kind of hell?

LORD: No sir.

GOODWIN: And this woman is wealthy and you've done—done this stuff to her and she's not raising any kind of hell?

LORD: No sir she didn't. She was just as cooperative and meek as she could be.

GOODWIN: Okay and what reason was it that she was that way?

LORD: I don't know except maybe she was afraid. I really don't know.

GOODWIN: Did she look afraid?

LORD: I don't know how she looked because again I grabbed her by the neck and pushed her head down.

GOODWIN: She's in the chair, you've taken the pillow case off her head. . .

LORD: In the chair?

GOODWIN: You put tape around her eyes. . .

LORD: In the chair, are we talking about how she looked in the chair?

GOODWIN: Un-huh. Did she ever say, "Charles, don't hurt me, Charles don't kill me?" The only thing she ever said is, "Charles I can't breathe?"

LORD: Going up the steps she said, "Charles I can't breathe," or, "I can't breathe," and I said as soon as I get you where I'm going to put you, I'll take it off. And then when I put her in the chair, ah I told her, "Don't make a sound, you speak when you're spoken to and everything will be okay, I don't want to hurt you."

GOODWIN: How long had you been going to the Eads Church?

LORD: Since about 1984.

GOODWIN: And how long has she been going there?

LORD: I don't know exactly but some time before that time.

GOODWIN: So since 1984, she knew that you were a church going man and she knew you and she knew your wife, she knew your home, and ah, so it didn't shock her that here you are, you've done taken her from her house and done these things to her?

LORD: Sir, I don't know whether it shocked her or not.

GOODWIN: And she trusted you. Did she trust you?

LORD: I think so until she until I grabbed her and told her that I'd hurt her if she made a sound.

GOODWIN: But she never offered any resistance?

LORD: No.

GOODWIN: She didn't scream out?

LORD: No sir, she never screamed.

GOODWIN: Everything at that point was going as planned? In other words, so far I hadn't heard any problems other than the fact that Sylvia is at home.

LORD: Believe it or not she never screamed. It went better than I thought it would. She was just as meek as a lamb she really was. She never cried out at all.

GOODWIN: All right this is 10:15, 10:20 A.M. in the morning around about 10:30 maybe with the taping of the eyes and all this?

LORD: Yes sir.

GOODWIN: All right. Go ahead. What happened next?

LORD: Well, after I, after I did that, I told her I had to go in the next room and ah, I would be back in just a minute and if she made a sound, ah, that would be the end of her. I might have said I'll kill you or something, I don't know.

GOODWIN: Did she ever ask you not to kill her?

LORD: No.

GOODWIN: Now surely you'd remember.

LORD: I think, I think she. . .

GOODWIN: Surely you can remember what it was that you said that impressed this millionaire.

LORD: I'm telling you just, just what happened· I think probably Doe was in such a state of shock and so confused, she didn't know what was going on.

GOODWIN: Did she ever say anything about needing medicine?

LORD: No.

GOODWIN: Up to the point we're at?

LORD: No.

GOODWIN: She never warned you about any medical conditions up to the point that we're at?

LORD: No not that I remember.

GOODWIN: What did you know about her medical condition? Everybody that. . .

LORD: I, I, I. . .

GOODWIN: Go ahead.

LORD: I knew, I knew she had an asthmatic condition or I had been told she had an asthmatic condition and that she was on some sort of prescription or whatnot for that.

GOODWIN: And also wasn't it common knowledge around the church and everybody she associated with that they couldn't, they had much difficulty operating on her eyes because they covered her head?

LORD: I didn't hear that.

GOODWIN: You didn't you didn't know that part?

LORD: No, I didn't know that.

GOODWIN: Okay all right go ahead.

LORD: Well after I, after I told her that and, ah, she said no sir I won't make a sound, I went downstairs and, ah, my wife was busy doing something making beds or whatever and I told her I'm back and, ah, I said I've got I've got some things to take out of the truck. I'll be back in a few minutes and she said okay lunch is about ready or would be ready shortly, I went back upstairs and in the bureau drawer, the top drawer, I had already positioned some sleeping pills that

I had, had from, now I'm not sure about this. I believe the doctor gave me when I had my back operated on in January of '90. . .

GOODWIN: Who's he, what's his name?

LORD: Ah, Dr. David Donahue and it was, ah, Methodist North in January of 1990. And I had some pain pills that, ah, I had left over from, ah—there's a Medi-Quick or drive-in type thing in Bartlett across from the Vickers Station, in 1986 or '7. I had a problem with an ear infection and they did give me those and I remember how woozy they had made me and I had several of those left, Anyway, I had positioned those things up there. My idea was to give her those to keep her quiet. So when I went back upstairs, ah, I believe I had a coke. There is a small refrigerator in the bathroom closet that we plug in from time to time because I spend a lot of time up there for reading and just for privacy, ah, I had a glass of Coke, I believe and I gave her several sleeping pills and maybe two or three of the pain pills, I'm not sure how many I gave her.

GOODWIN: No, problem giving them to her, she just took them?

LORD: No, she, "No, no," she said. I said, "Ah, take these because, ah, I don't trust you not to be quiet," and she said, "I promise you I'll be quiet." and I said," No you, you're to take these or I'm going to have to knock you unconscious, bust you in the head." So she said, "I'll take them."

GOODWIN: She never, never asked you what you wanted?

LORD: Well, I'm not certain but at that time she might have said what's going on or whatnot but I just answered her with be quiet, ah, you'll know later, ah, she never offered any resistance·

GOODWIN: Without any resistance. . .

LORD: It went better than I thought it really, it really did.

GOODWIN: Well I can understand and it looks to me like it went better but I still, I don't want to forget and I want to ask you one more time about here's somebody that's offering no resistance· I don't, I don't know why you taped her eyes and not her mouth. Here it is, you've got a perfect opportunity, your wife's at home, here's this lady, you have no idea what she might do, so we're going to tape her eyes and we're going not to tape her mouth· Here's a man that's 59 years old and has made a good living all his life at a high position in the Federal Government is looking at this lady he just kidnapped and we're going to tape her eyes where she can't see what's she's already seen, but we're not going to tape her mouth so that she can't make no noise.

LORD: She hadn't seen that much because I had a pillow case over her over her head. And when I took her upstairs and sat her in the chair, I told her to sit there and I immediately took a piece of duct tape and I told her to close her eyes. I took the tape I took the pillow case off and taped her eyes. I don't know why I did that but I guess it was because I didn't want her looking at me.

GOODWIN: That's why I might was going to suggest not being a psychologist that maybe you couldn't take her looking at you. . .

LORD: I couldn't.

GOODWIN: Because of what you had done or there could be other reasons· Maybe you wasn't concerned with her making any noise and screaming and hollering for help but you was concerned more with what she might see other than what she had already seen. She seen you, it's a possibility she knew she you was at your house.

LORD: I don't think she did. And she kept assuring me she was, she was, she was so cooperative·

GOODWIN: Un-huh.

LORD: She said, ah, and I told her I was going to the next room and I said if you make any noise, I'm going to bust you in the head. I'm going to hurt you.

GOODWIN: I understand.

LORD: She assured she wouldn't.

GOODWIN: But isn't it possible that you didn't care whether she made a lot of noise and hollered and screamed and raised hell?

LORD: Oh, you bet there is.

GOODWIN: That there wasn't anybody on your property that you cared knowing that she at that. . .

LORD: Oh no, no, my wife was at home.

GOODWIN: That's what I'm talking about. Maybe you didn't care that your wife knew she was up there.

LORD: On no. sir, no way, and no.

GOODWIN: But we taped her eyes and not her mouth?

LORD: That's right.

GOODWIN: And you were worried that your wife might find out that she's up there?

LORD: Yes I was.

GOODWIN: And we're going we're going to stick to that.

LORD: Yes.

GOODWIN: Taped her eyes and not her mouth?

LORD: I did put a gag in her mouth but I took it off.

GOODWIN: Where was that at?

LORD: That was when I sat her in the chair. I, I, I started to gag her but she said something about I can't breathe and I said okay, you be, you're going to be quiet now, you promise me you're going to be quiet, and that's what happened.

GOODWIN: Okay. Well maybe I'll not ask questions so fast because when I raise the issue of what she saw, then we remember that we put a pillowcase on her head. And I raise the issue of the tape over her eyes and not her mouth and now we remember that we did gag her.

LORD: I started to gag her.

GOODWIN: Okay. All right go ahead from there. What happened next?

LORD: Well that was when I first took her up there.

GOODWIN: The pills, we were at the pills.

LORD: Okay, ah, I told her to take these pills and again I don't remember how many there were of them but there were, there were several and she, she said, I said, "Take these," and she said, "what are they?" and I said, "They're, they're pills that I want you to take," and she said, "Will they hurt me?" and I said, "No." She said, "Well I promise I won't make a sound, I'll, and I'll do whatever you want." Ah, I said, and I said, "You don't have an option. It's either that or I'm going to bust you in the head and knock you unconscious," so she took the pills. I put them in her hand, she put them in her mouth maybe two at a time, and I handed her the glass of Coke and she, she downed them.

GOODWIN: Just not to get off course. Why are we doing this?

LORD: Why are we doing this?

GOODWIN: Un-huh, the whole thing, starting at the house, making the phone call posing as Sam Wagner, why are we doing this? What is our motive for the, for the point we're at now?

LORD: Money.

GOODWIN: And how did you hope to obtain money by what you've done?

LORD: I hoped to obtain a ransom for her.

GOODWIN: From who?

LORD: From her husband.

GOODWIN: And successful or not, what, what did you think ---you'd agree a success would be? What was the percentage that you thought that Alan Roberts might pay?

LORD: Pretty good.

GOODWIN: Percentage high?

LORD: Yeah, high percentage.

GOODWIN: Based on what assumption?

LORD: Well, based on the assumption that they've been together forty some-odd years, ah, they were at church together most of the time, ah. . .

GOODWIN: So now we're at this situation. We've got motive, we'll accept that. I think that's pretty well set out in all your statements that it was for money, okay. Ah, we've got her and we've got her up to the house now and we've got her taking pills. She's still alive, if the ransom's paid and it's not paid, as far as Mrs. Roberts is concerned, I mean what's her, ah, what's her outlook at that point in time? What are we going to do with her?

LORD: I thought two things. First of all, I thought that I might collect the money and reason with Doe. But then. . .

GOODWIN: Statement #1?

LORD: I don't remember. But then I had also planned because I had dug that pit earlier that if all that failed, I would have to dispose of her.

GOODWIN: But the pit was dug to put her in if all else failed?

LORD: Yes, yes.

GOODWIN: The same one we took her body out of?

LORD: Yes.

GOODWIN: And just to hurry up and speed over some things, there never was two pits there?

LORD: Not that. . .

GOODWIN: There was always one?

LORD: Well. . .

GOODWIN: Or we just had one about a week or two weeks prior to kidnapping her?

LORD: Yeah. I had, well, I did, I did turn that compost but instead of digging down as deep as I did, I would dig down about six inches and turn it.

GOODWIN: The hole that we took her out of, is the hole that was dug prior to her kidnapping to put her in if all things failed?

LORD: Yes sir, that's right.

GOODWIN: Okay, we've got her drugged and whatever. She's done taken the pills and, ah, let's take it, pick it up from there. What happened next?

LORD: I stayed up there oh maybe 15 minutes. I sat in the chair, ah, facing her. She was, and I, and I, after maybe 15, 20 minutes I'm not sure, I was talking to her and I could tell she was under the effects of the pills. Her speech was slurred. You know she was slow to answer that, that kind of thing. So to avoid any suspicion, I went back downstairs. I had lunch and I sat in my chair like, I like I do usually after lunch thinking about what time to go, ah, call Alan Roberts. A little bit later, I went back upstairs to, ah, to check on her and she was sound to sleep. If I can explain it, her hands were tied to the chair, her feet were tied to the chair, ah the belt was around her and she was sort of slumped this way and her nose was running all the way down so, I mean, she was, you know, she was, she was out. So I, I checked her legs and it looked like the circulation was being off of her legs and her hands. I untied her, ah, laid her on the bed, completely disrobed her, then I retied her hands and her feet and I could I could move her and tell that, you know, she was unconscious or asleep out of it. That's when I cut the buttons, ah, I'm not sure whether the buttons were on the blouse or the skirt, I, I don't remember, but anyway I cut the buttons off and then the, ah, the metal fasteners on the bra, I cut those off. She had some kind of pen on her blouse, I took it off and I put the metal, those metal parts in my pocket.

I took the metal the things that wouldn't burn out of the, ah, out of the purse and put those in my pocket. Then I stuffed her clothing and her purse in a plastic garbage bag that I had, a couple of bags upstairs. I went, ah, let's see, I don't think, I put those I put those things in the closet. Then I went back downstairs and this must have been this is getting on 2:00 or so I suppose, I'm not sure about the time. I went back down to the garage and I put the, ah, the metal parts the pill box, the buttons, the lipstick whatever else I figured wouldn't burn, into a paper sack on the work bench in the garage behind my toolbox. Let's see, then I, I think I went back upstairs to check on her and she, and she hadn't moved.

GOODWIN: You hadn't done anything with the pill bottles because you thought you might need them again?

LORD: I still had some left and I did use them again.

GOODWIN: You did use them again?

LORD: Yes.

GOODWIN: And did you use them all?

LORD: No. I threw the rest of them away later though.

GOODWIN: What about the bottles?

LORD: The bottles too. I think I burned the bottles.

GOODWIN: You threw the pills away and then burned the bottles?

LORD: Yeah, the plastic bottles that pills come in?

GOODWIN: Un-huh.

LORD: 'You know I burned those. I'm pretty sure I did.

GOODWIN: Okay go ahead.

LORD: They were in the, they were in the bureau drawer and when I when I cleaned out, I cleaned out, yeah, I put the bottles in the, in the sack with the purse and the clothing

GOODWIN: And we're sure we're not getting mixed up with Statement #2 when we were talking about the pillow and the smothering and we took her clothes and put them in our pocket?

LORD: NO, no.

GOODWIN: You remember saying that?

LORD: Yeah. That was when I said I was in her house.

GOODWIN: Right.

LORD: And on her bed and that wasn't true.

GOODWIN: Okay. You're clear about this? All the clothes taken off and the metal at your house?

LORD: Yes, she was stark naked.

GOODWIN: Okay.

LORD: Where was I? I had gone downstairs and I put the put the metal things, the metal parts in a, ah, paper sack and I put them behind my toolbox on the, on the work bench. Then I went back upstairs, ah, to check on her again and she hadn't moved. Ah, I really thought I had given her too much and I, I probably did. Ah, I went back in the house and it was, I don't know getting on toward 2:00 I suppose, and I think I probably told my wife I had some things to do our in the garage, ah, ah, but anyway I went, I went back out in the garage and sort of tinkered around and whatnot. I was waiting to, ah, to call Alan Roberts. For some reason I had said in my mind that I would call him and I don't remember the time, ah either 3:00 or I don't remember. You know some, some set time in my mind was when I was going to call him. So then I told my wife that I had had to go back to either Central Hardware or Ace Hardware somewhere to pick up something and, ah, I just told her I was leaving so, so she said okay. And I had locked the apartment door.

GOODWIN: Did she really make any comments to you about the weather?

[Goodwin is referring to statements in a previous confession.]

LORD: Well, she, she, she kept telling me that it was hot out in the garage and you know I really ought to come in because I did have a heat stroke about a year or two earlier and I told her there was some things that I wanted to clean up and some things I was working on and I was always out there tinkering.

GOODWIN: You're telling her you're leaving the house and you're telling her that you're going to work in the compost pile and she says it's too hot out there for that. That's before you're leaving the house?

LORD: I wasn't working in the compost pile. That was a lie too.

GOODWIN: And that was on, that was on the second statement but you fully remember making that statement you told her you was going to work on a compost pile and she says it's too hot outside for that? You remember telling them that in the statement?

LORD: Yes.

GOODWIN: Clearly?

LORD: Yes.

GOODWIN: And that's not true?

LORD: That's not true.

GOODWIN: Okay.

LORD: I told her I had some things to do outside and she said, "It's too hot," and I said, "Well, I'm going to be in the, mostly in the garage, you know, just, just passed off something and I won't get too hot. I'll, I'll be fine."

GOODWIN: It's 2:00 or so in the afternoon?

LORD: Yeah.

GOODWIN: She's asleep in the garage apartment?

LORD: Right.

GOODWIN: And your wife is still working in the house?

LORD: Yeah.

GOODWIN: And you're fixing to leave?

LORD: It was some time after 2:00, I'm not sure. I tinkered around for a while killing time trying to decide when to go make my phone call. So when I went back upstairs and, ah, checked on her again and she was still out but she was able to, able to mumble, so I sat her up and gave her two more pills. I waited a few minutes. I went back downstairs and I told my wife I had to run to either Central Hardware or Ace Hardware I needed something and, you know, she never questioned me about when I work in the garage and what I do, I'm always tinkering building something, and I said I'll be right back. So I locked the, ah, locked the garage apartment. There's only one key and I had it in my pocket and I tore off to, ah, to Bartlett and I went to a phone booth there at, ah, just north of, ah, 64 and 70. I think it's a Horde's or a Burger King. There's a phone booth out in the parking lot and that's when I called Allen Roberts. And I disguised my voice and I said, ah, something like, ah, we have your wife and, ah, if you don't, if you call the police or the FBI, I'm not sure of my words here, ah; we are going to crush her skull. I wanted it to sound like it was a gang rather than Just an individual. Ah, and you, ah, I want you right now to go out in your front, out in your front yard, your side yard and crush your recording machine, your tape, I

186

might have told him to burn it, I'm not, I'm not sure, because we're watching.

GOODWIN: And you knew he had a tape machine on his phone?

LORD: No, but I just suspected that he did. I really didn't know that.

GOODWIN: Okay.

LORD: Let's see.

GOODWIN: You don't remember your exact words but you know you told him not to call the police?

LORD: Yes I did.

GOODWIN: And you threatened harm to his wife if he didn't comply?

LORD: I did.

GOODWIN: Go ahead.

LORD: And I told him to get a hundred thousand dollars ready, and the truth is by that time, I was shaking, I was so scared that I hung the phone up and left and I got maybe a quarter of a mile down the road and realized that I didn't tell him where to take the money. But I didn't, I didn't go back. I thought, well, I'll just wait to see if in fact he calls the police and what happens and I'll just go from there. So that's when everything started to started to come apart.

GOODWIN: And that's what time now?

LORD: I'm not sure but around 3:00.

GOODWIN: Un-huh.

LORD: Between 3:00 and 4:00 some somewhere in that time frame.

[The time of the ransom call Lord describes is not substantiated. We speculate that perhaps Lord did make a

187

call between two and three, but Allen did not return home until around 4 p.m. At that point Allen made the calls to his wife's friend, including Sylvia Lord. Then around 5:00 p.m. Allen received what may have been Lord's second call. The absence of Agent Overall and Insp. Swain is sorely felt here. No one in the room at this moment has any knowledge of the chronology of that Friday. The reader is advised to take Lord's times with a block of salt.]

GOODWIN: Okay and then you went back home?

LORD: I went back home.

GOODWIN: Okay go ahead.

LORD: Ah, I went in the house and fixed myself a glass of, ah, ice coffee, instant ice coffee. Ah, I don't remember what my wife was doing. I think she said something like, "Well, did you get what you wanted?" and I said yeah I, I'll be back in a few minutes, I'm going out here and do whatever I told her I was I was doing and, ah, I went I went back upstairs. I went back upstairs and, ah, [Mrs. Roberts] was, ah, still out of it. I came back downstairs after about 15 minutes or so and it was shortly after that, as I remember that, ah Allen Roberts called and my wife answered the phone and he wanted to know if, ah, if she had seen Doe.

GOODWIN: What time was this?

LORD: I don't know between 4:00 and 5:00 somewhere along in there.

GOODWIN: What time did he report it to the Police Department?

LORD: I don't know.

[Why there wasn't a follow up on the fact that Lord is saying the ransom call was made around 3:00 p.m. and Allen called the Lord's house between 3:00 and 4:00 p.m.

188

and didn't report the kidnapping till after 5:00 pm.
Obviously Goodwin isn't comfortable with what he's hearing
but doesn't pursue it.]

GOODWIN: What time did he come home and find that she wasn't there?

LORD: I don't know but, ah, according to the paper and what I heard later, he came home at lunchtime, ah, and she wasn't there but didn't think too much about it and, ah, then he left again. That's what I either read or heard. . . called and talked to my wife.

GOODWIN: Didn't talk to you?

LORD: No. And the conversation was something like, ah, what my wife told me that, ah, have you seen Doe and she said no. He said, well, he had come home and she wasn't there. Something like it wasn't like her and Sylvia assured him that well she's just probably off with somebody. Ah, I don't think I'd worry but if she doesn't show up in a little while, you call me, and, ah, she said he said that that he would.

But then finished, finished that up I guess it was 7:30, 8:00 ah, hadn't heard anything, so my wife called over there and I believe she said she talked to, ah, the niece, Brenda Keith. I think, but anyway one of the nieces answered the phone and, ah, Sylvia told her what had happened, just wanted to be sure everything was okay and my wife told me that Brenda said, "Well I'm sure everything's okay. Ah, so [my wife] said, "Well, okay, thanks a lot," and you know that was the end of that.

GOODWIN: Okay.

LORD: The first that, we heard, you know, my wife heard the next morning I guess it was around 10:00, a neighbor, Marilyn Pulltam, called and I believe I answered the phone then and she said Charles, have you heard that

Doe Roberts has been kidnapped, and I said something like oh my goodness no yak, yak, yak. She said, "Well they're not, they're asking everybody not to call the house because the F.B.I. is over there and you know all this good kind of stuff. So ah. . .

GOODWIN: So that was a pretty good pipe line. He's already done what you told him not to do?

LORD: Yeah.

GOODWIN: Just several hours after you got home, you verified that, he's done. . .

LORD: No, this was, this was the next morning about 10:00. I'm skipping over to, try to. . .

GOODWIN: Okay go ahead. We're, we're on August the 8th at 10:00?

LORD: Yeah, that was when. . .

GOODWIN: And we know the F.B.I. is on the case?

LORD: That's right.

GOODWIN: Okay.

LORD: That's right, sure did. Okay, to back up, let's see, after I got home and Alan called, ah, I made, ah, I guess made another trip upstairs to, ah, to see that she was still asleep or, or whatnot and then I. . .

GOODWIN: Yeah. I was wondering when you was going back upstairs in the apartment to see check on her or see if she was still there.

LORD: Well, I was, I was in and out of there I guess maybe, the longest period of time I didn't check on her was probably the 45 minutes it took round trip to, ah, to tear into Bartlett and make the phone call and get back.

GOODWIN: Okay so. . .

LORD: I was up there every, maybe, I don't, know 20 minutes, half hour, whatnot. I would, I had gotten pretty comfortable with the fact that the pills were working and she was she was just out of it.

GOODWIN: Okay now it's the next morning, 10:00 in the morning?

LORD: No, no, no, no, no, let's, let's finish this up. It was getting toward, toward dinner time. Then so I got her up and, ah, put her back in the chair and tied her. I didn't, I didn't gag her because she was, she was just out of it. She couldn't even moan and, ah, I did put a blanket around her because I had taken all her clothes off and I had satisfied myself that everything was going to be okay.

So I went back downstairs and, ah, I don't remember what time this was and we had dinner and, ah, we watched TV for a little while I guess and then I went back out in the garage to tinker. Actually I went back upstairs to check and, ah, she was, she was still out of it. So then I went back downstairs and, ah, my wife is one that goes to bed early and I'll stay up most of the times till 12:00 or 1:00. So she went to bed. I guess I told her---I usually stay up at night and watch the Discovery Channel or some documentaries and she went to bed sometime before 10:00 and I had the TV on in there. I kind of turned it down.

After I was sure that she had, ah, she had gone to sleep, I'd say maybe another 45 minutes and this must be must be getting close to 11:00, I went back upstairs and, ah, I untied her from the chair and put her in the, put her in the bed and, ah, covered her up.

(Answer Continued): She was beginning to, ah, sort of come out of it sort of speak she could, she could make sense, does that make sense? She could answer me when I would, I would talk to her and I said, ah, how long will it take Alan to come up with a hundred thousand dollars in cash and she mumbled something like maybe, maybe an hour or two. Later I find out that they kept that much cash at least that much cash in the house but I didn't know that at the time. So I sat down in the chair and I believe I smoked a cigarette, ah, trying to decide where to go from there. Ah, I tried to talk to her and, ah, I had really overdosed her on the, on the sleeping pills and the pain pills.

By that time, I was I was getting afraid that, ah, somebody might come around, you know, I didn't, I didn't know what to do. So I went back down to the landing by the sun porch and looked in and, ah, my wife was, her light was still off in her bedroom and there was nobody in the, in the den. I walked up to the den and looked in the window. So I went back upstairs. . .

[Lord gives a brief description of the sexual activity with Mrs. Roberts in a comatose state.]

After that, I gave her the rest of the pills. All total I can't tell you how many I had but, ah, I gave her all but maybe three or four out of each bottle and I thought that, I thought that might finish her off.

I went back downstairs and now, we're talking, I don't know somewhere around midnight, I'm not certain, and everything is still, still cool in the house. I do remember tip-toeing down the hall to, to check and sometimes my wife will go to bed with a little portable radio on but it was off so I knew she was, she was asleep. So I went back upstairs and I smothered [Mrs. Roberts] with a pillow.

GOODWIN: The same as in the second statement, September 1st?

LORD: I suppose.

GOODWIN: Do you recall in that statement. . .

LORD: Except in that statement I said I did that at her house.

GOODWIN: Right. But the smothering of the pillow in the second statement, that was true?

LORD: Yes.

GOODWIN: Okay. You said you thought the pills would finish her off?

LORD: Yeah.

GOODWIN: What does that mean?*

LORD: Rather than me having to do something physical to her because that was, I don't know, it was repulsive to me but apparently I didn't have any trouble doing it later.

[Goodwin reviews Lord's statement about the sexual activity to provide the ground work that Mrs. Roberts was in no condition to give her consent despite what Lord might have said. There is still speculation about this part of the confession. There was medical testimony offered later as to the fact of Lord's impotence. Then Goodwin spends tine clarifying statements made in the previous two confessions and then resumes the description of the murder.]

LORD: After I, after I smothered her and I knew she was dead, I picked her up over my shoulder. No. I went back downstairs to check to be sure that everything was still cool, came back up, I put her over my shoulder. I remember her being very heavy and, ah, I took her out through the garage to the pit.

GOODWIN: Un-huh.

LORD: And, ah, put her in it. I came back to the shed with a wheel barrow and got two sacks of, ah. . .

GOODWIN: Wait a minute. What time is this?

LORD: This is probably 12:30.

GOODWIN: At, we've had her since about 10:15 that morning?

LORD: Yeah, yeah.

GOODWIN: And she's in the pit now and how long has she been dead?

LORD: Fifteen minutes at the most.

GOODWIN: She's in the pit?

LORD: Un-huh.

GOODWIN: Exactly like I found her the other day and these other gentlemen and your attorney found her the other day?

LORD: I don't know how you found her but when I put her in, she was flat on her back with her hands this way.

GOODWIN: Okay. Let's, let's assume for argument sake that nobody's tampered with that thing since you put her in and she was taken out and your lawyer was there when she was taken out. She's been dead 15 minutes, she's in the pit, then she's covered up as we'll get into later, and nobody's tampered with her until she was removed the other day at your house?

LORD: I did not tamper with her and no nobody did.

GOODWIN: You never touched her again?

LORD: No sir.

GOODWIN: After you put her in the pit?

LORD: No, no.

GOODWIN: And what we found is what you saw before you covered her up?

LORD: Yes.

GOODWIN: Okay and then you immediately went to your shed, I suppose, to go ahead and cover her up, right?

LORD: I went to the shed to get the two sacks of lime.

GOODWIN: Un-huh.

LORD: And a shovel, okay.

GOODWIN: Un-huh.

LORD: I went; it's only about what 10, 15 yards up there to the pit?

GOODWIN: Un-huh.

LORD: Ah, the dirt had been piled up on this side of the compost pile. You could only see the holes from the back side over there.

GOODWIN: Un-huh.

LORD: Ah, I broke the, the two sacks, I think there were two sacks, open and, ah, very quickly shoveled it and sprinkled it around you know. I don't know whether I put the sacks in the pit or not. I think I burned the sacks later that next day also. But then I just shoveled some dirt, ah, in there and maybe some leaves. I went back upstairs, ah, got the sack I had put the purse, excuse me, and the clothes in and the pill, pill bottles, came back downstairs and put them in the garage, ah, on the far side over there by the by the compressor.

GOODWIN: Un-huh.

LORD: Then I went in the house and went to bed.

GOODWIN: And she's in the hole?

LORD: She's in the hole.

GOODWIN: And what's on top of her now that when you went to bed?

LORD: The, ah, ah, the lime and a little bit of dirt and, ah, leaves.

GOODWIN: Did you ever later put anymore lime on her; we'll cut to the chase.

LORD: No, no, no. The, the next, the next day, I don't remember whether it was that morning or that afternoon, I told my wife I needed to work on, work on the compost pile so it was either earlier in the morning or more than likely late afternoon when it had cooled off some. I went back out there with the manure fork I got the leaves out.

GOODWIN: You got the leaves out?

LORD: I pitched them back. . .

GOODWIN: Pitched them back out of the grave.

LORD: Back up onto the, onto the, to the mound there, looking around all the time, and I, then I don't believe I put anymore lime but I'm not certain but I did go back to the shed and get I don't know how many bags of ready-mix, okay

GOODWIN: Un-huh, how long did it take you to dig that hole?

LORD: I dug the hole about a week or so before and I guess it probably took me off and on a couple of hours at the most. I didn't dig it all at one time.

GOODWIN: Did you have any problem digging it?

LORD: The only problem I had was, ah, a couple of roots.

GOODWIN: And these roots that you had problems with were they at the feet of Mrs. Roberts or were they at her head as you as you recall placing her in the grave?

LORD: I think probably the bigger root was at the Foot because I remember the pit kind of narrowed back there.

GOODWIN: Did she fit in there when you put her in there?

LORD: Yeah, yeah. As I remember. . .

GOODWIN: You didn't do anymore digging to the pit after you put her in there?

LORD: No, no.

GOODWIN: So when you encountered the root that you had all the trouble with digging, did you know that the pit had to be longer? Did you measure it with a measuring stick?

LORD: I had measured the pit. It was about, ah, two and a half or three feet wide and about, ah, six feet long, roughly.

GOODWIN: But at the root that you had problems with, what did you do to make it long enough for her since you couldn't get through the root?

LORD: I, I believe part of the roots were sticking out and I used sharp shooter. Do you know what a sharp shooter is?

GOODWIN: Un-huh.

LORD: To, ah, to cut some of the roots. I don't think I cut I cut most of them. There was another root I believe toward the head but I didn't have any trouble with that. But when I put her in there, ah, I just more or less dropped her in.

GOODWIN: Un-huh.

LORD: And, ah, it seemed to fit you know.

GOODWIN: You didn't have to dig anymore?

LORD: No, I didn't dig anymore.

GOODWIN: You didn't dig around any roots because you couldn't dig through them?

LORD: I don't remember digging. . .

GOODWIN: So before you sealed this grave, how many hours are you talking about from the time that you put her in there until, you came back later and finished the job the next afternoon after it got cool? How many hours are we talking about?

LORD: Probably less than ah hour.

GOODWIN: From the time you put her in there, then an hour later it was sealed the way we found it?

LORD: No, no, no, no, no you see when I put her in there. . .

GOODWIN: Uh-huh.

LORD: That night, 12:30 or so in the in the morning, I put, I put the lime in there.

GOODWIN: Uh-huh.

LORD: And I might have shoveled a little dirt I'm not sure, then I pulled the leaves in.

GOODWIN: Right. Then you came back later.

LORD: Yeah.

GOODWIN: And finished the job.

LORD: Right.

GOODWIN: How many hours was that?

LORD: To finish it?

GOODWIN: Uh-huh. What I saw and these gentlemen saw. . .

LORD: Less, less than an hour.

GOODWIN: You went in the house and went to bed?

LORD: Yeah.

GOODWIN: And in less than an hour you were back?

LORD: No, no, no, no, no, no, no. I didn't come back. It was either that morning 8:00 or 9:00, I think it was Saturday afternoon okay.

GOODWIN: All right that's what I followed you. So how many hours from the time she was put in there until the concrete was laid on top of the grave?

LORD: Oh, okay. I put the concrete on the grave Saturday afternoon.

GOODWIN: And the dirt and the concrete kind of all

198

went at the same time?

LORD: Yeah as I remember, I kind of mixed it.

GOODWIN: And that's how many hours?

LORD: I'm not — the actual burying process?

GOODWIN: No, the whole time.

LORD: Oh the whole time.

GOODWIN: How long had she been laying there when you, from the time you put her in there and you walked away and never went back out there again, when the burying process was over, how many hours was she there?

LORD: I still don't understand your question. Let me tell you this. I put her in there about 12:30 and partially covered everything up, okay.

GOODWIN: Right 12:30 AM?

LORD: AM. I came in the house and went to bed and the next afternoon I would say it was sometime around 5:00 or 6:00. . .

GOODWIN: So 12:30 AM, 12:30 PM that afternoon she would have been in there twelve hours approximately?

LORD: Right, right.

GOODWIN: So then at 5:00, let's say for instance, would have been approximately 16 1/2 hours?

LORD: That's about right.

GOODWIN: Before the Final grave was covered, the dirt, the concrete?

LORD: Yes sir that's right.

GOODWIN: And during the course of those 16 hours, all she had on her was lime and some debris or leaves or trash from the pile?

LORD: Yes.

GOODWIN: That was all that was on top of her?

LORD: Yes.

GOODWIN: For 16 hours?

LORD: Yeah.

[This line of questioning arises from the attitude of Mrs. Roberts' hands in the grave—their position seemed to suggest that there was movement after burial. Lord's description of her position did not settle this question. Lord appears to have no idea about Goodwin's intent during these questions. The truth is that, after death, there could have been some muscular changes due to the onset and passing away of rigor mortis, hence Goodwin's question about length of time.]

GOODWIN: Okay do ya'll want to take a break? I'm going; this is the second tape that's on the tape recorder now. They're not finished but when we start over again, I'm going to use new tapes and the time is 4:10. This will be the continuation of the statement of Charles Lord. It will be the third tape taken into evidence at 4:20 PM. Mr. Lord, when we finished, we had established that we're talking about approximately 16 1/2 hours from the time that she, the victim, was first placed in the grave until it was sealed in the manner in which the Sheriff's Department found it, and that's true, approximately 16 1/2 hours?

LORD: Yeah, yes that's true. When I when I first put her in the pit that early that morning or late that night whichever you want to call it, as I remember there were two or maybe three sacks of lime, and they're 40 pound sacks, there might, there might have been one sack of concrete I don't remember but I did make just one trip with the wheelbarrow so I don't believe there were more than three sacks of, ah, one or, or the other and I shoveled in on, in on the body and, ah, then just pulled the leaves in and ah went in and went to bed.

GOODWIN: As best you could you took the leaves out the next day?

LORD: Yeah I used a manure fork and, ah, got most of the leaves out the next day. I. . .

GOODWIN: You filled it with dirt and then capped it with concrete?

LORD: Well, as, as I remember when I, when, when the dirt was up on the compost pile, you couldn't help but mix the dirt with, with the leaves and I'm not certain but I believe, well I knew, I know, I used the hoe because I could pull it in quicker and get, get through quicker. I pulled in some dirt and leaves and then put some concrete in. I'm, I'm not sure how I how I did that mix but ah. . .

GOODWIN: Have you ever opened the grave?

LORD: No.

GOODWIN: Have you ever seen the grave?

LORD: Have I ever seen it?

GOODWIN: Remove the compost on top of it and looked at it?

LORD: No.

GOODWIN: Curiosity, worry, possibly?

LORD: No, no, no, no. As a as a matter fact, ah, early that fall when the leaves begun began to fall, we have a riding mower with a with a grass catcher and I piled the leaves even higher up to the top of the fence and what you saw was, was a settling effect of those leaves from the prior, the prior fall.

GOODWIN: All right the sexual incident with the victim was after you talked to Alan Roberts on the phone in Bartlett, right?

LORD: Yes.

GOODWIN: And he told you on the phone to go jump in the river over that money for her?

LORD: No he didn't.

GOODWIN: He didn't say anything on the phone when you called him that upset you and it was taken out on Mrs. Roberts?

LORD: No sir. No, he didn't, no. I don't remember. He was not, ah, he was, not angry. He didn't tell me to go to hell or jump in the river. Ah, he said something like, oh me, well just tell me what to do.

GOODWIN: Okay. And the only other person that knows about this is you and the law enforcement people and your lawyer?

LORD: That's true.

GOODWIN: There's not another person in your family that knows about this?

LORD: Well I don't know what you mean by "I was afraid of her" because I wasn't afraid of her.

GOODWIN: She didn't know anything on you?

LORD: No.

GOODWIN: She didn't know about the church money?

LORD: No sir, no.

GOODWIN: And you wasn't afraid that that's why she was spending so much time at the church and talking to the minister, that she found out about the money? She didn't know anything about the money you took from the church?

LORD: Not to my knowledge because the first time I took, ah, some was in February.

GOODWIN: Un-huh.

LORD: That was the first, okay. The rest was after August after all this, in October and I think in December.

GOODWIN: So that would prove anybody interested that the money from the church didn't have anything to do with this?

LORD: That's true.

GOODWIN: She didn't know about that?

LORD: No, no, I, I had. . .

GOODWIN: But you had thought about this some well before two weeks before she was kidnapped?

LORD: I hadn't thought about this specific thing.

GOODWIN: Un-huh.

LORD: But I was trying to figure, you see what was happening was I had a large loan at the credit union.

GOODWIN: Un-huh.

LORD: Okay and I was trying to figure some way to, to pay, keep paying that, okay?

GOODWIN: Un-huh.

LORD: And that's why the money disappeared in those parts that you know that disappeared, okay?

GOODWIN: Right. No that's wrong. See I don't know anything about that.

LORD: Okay.

GOODWIN: I don't want to know because I don't want to go too far past that. I just want to make it clear as we---in this statement right here that she didn't know that you was taking money from the church?

LORD: If she knew it, I didn't know it. Okay and I think the only way, no, anybody knew it, it would have been Hazel Richmond our Treasurer and Hazel, if Hazel had known or even suspected. . .

GOODWIN: Well how come why didn't we kidnap Hazel?

LORD: Well, because it wouldn't be any point in kidnapping Hazel, Hazel didn't have any money.

GOODWIN: Okay. So the bottom line on kidnapping Mrs. Roberts was the money like you said earlier?

LORD: Yes sir.

GOODWIN: No other reason?

LORD: No other reason.

GOODWIN: And she was selected as your victim because she had money?

LORD: That's right.

GOODWIN: And you knew she had money?

LORD: Yes.

GOODWIN: In other words you had heard that they were millionaires?

LORD: Yes.

GOODWIN: And when she, the day you put her in the church at her house. . .

LORD: In the church?

GOODWIN: Correction, in your truck.

LORD: Yeah.

GOODWIN: At her house, it wasn't any way in hell she was ever coming home that day? There wasn't any way she was coming home? You don't take long to dig no damn hole and you live in the country, it doesn't take long to dig no hole. You don't have to dig no hole two weeks prior to getting the victim. It doesn't take but a few minutes to dig a hole. When you, she left her house that day, there was no way that woman was coming home. She hadn't been in your custody and you'd already had sex with her, a millionaire's wife. Prior to having sex with her, you done took her clothes off, you done took all the buttons off her clothes, already planning to destroy those prior to ever having the sex with her. . .

LORD: Well you. . .

GOODWIN: That woman wasn't going home.

LORD: Are you asking me or telling me?

GOODWIN: I'm asking you.

LORD: Oh okay.

GOODWIN: She wasn't going home. She was going to a hole on Great Oaks Road in Fayette County, Tennessee the day she got in your truck at her house?

LORD: That's not necessarily true.

GOODWIN: In what way is it not necessarily true?

LORD: Because until I realized that I had overdosed her, I really had some hope in my mind, maybe not much okay, that I could that I could talk with Doe, explain the situation, and she would probably tell me as she would have if I had handled this correctly, I think ah, Charles, I'll help you, you know just let me go, we'll forget about this and we'll work it out. She was that kind of person.

GOODWIN: Well, why did you say in the statement #2 that most of that paragraph is true by your own statement that when you began talking about your financial problems, she became angry?

LORD: Well that was just a lie because. . .

GOODWIN: But it's a good lie. It plays it plays to the motive, it plays to money, and it plays to all of it. It fits right in except the fact that you say it's a lie. The rest of that paragraph is true.

LORD: Yeah. That part's not true.

GOODWIN: If she had played ball, what we talking about sexually and money, ah you, you can overwhelm her with your charm and all this is going to be all right and I'm going to take her back home? We done took all the buttons off so we can destroy them. We done dug the hole in the back yard. But it was only at the point where you felt like she was overdosed that you knew all was lost, that Doe Roberts was never going home again?

LORD: I think so. I really do.

GOODWIN: How many pills did you give her?

LORD: I don't know, ah, ah. . .

GOODWIN: What was the brand? What were they for, pain you said?

LORD: One was for pain when I had the ear infection and the others were capsules and I believe they were sleeping tablets but I'm ah. . .

GOODWIN: How many did the doctor prescribe you to take?

LORD: I don't remember.

GOODWIN: One a day? Do you remember if it was more than one a day? Do you remember if it was one for pain as needed?

LORD: I think the pain pills might have been for pain as needed and I believe the, ah, the others, the sleeping tablets were, ah, one or two a night.

GOODWIN: Several times during the course of this statement we're taking now, I noticed you said you thought you had give her too many, I knew by then I had give her too many, what point did you think you'd give her too many?

LORD: After I gave her the first several and, ah, realized how out of it she was.

GOODWIN: But she came back enough from the first pills you give her for you to sit down and talk to her?

LORD: To make some sense, yeah.

GOODWIN: How many times did Alan Roberts have dinner at your house since the kidnapping?. . . ..

LORD: I think twice.

GOODWIN: And how many times had he had dinner at your house prior to the kidnapping?

LORD: Once maybe.

GOODWIN: How many times had the victim, Doe Roberts, been to your house prior to the kidnapping?

LORD: I don't know ah. . .

GOODWIN: Would she average once a year?

LORD: Oh yeah, yeah.

GOODWIN: Okay and would she, did she ever work in your flower beds?

LORD: No.

GOODWIN: When she was there at your house, it was social or church related?

LORD: Church related. Like I remember she and some of the other ladies would come over oh late summer or early fall. The, ah, the woman's auxiliary would make things for, ah, the Methodist Church for example, stockings, red stockings for the mothers to take newborns home in at Christmas time. And they would cut those out and sew and it would be kind of a sewing circle type thing and they would be there maybe two or three hours doing that.

GOODWIN: Did she ever tell you that she was having problems with her husband?

LORD: No.

GOODWIN: Other than being a lie in the second statement that you gave September 1st, where did you come up with that at?

LORD: I got that impression.

GOODWIN: Prior to the kidnapping or afterwards?

LORD: Prior to the kidnapping.

GOODWIN: You got that impression?

LORD: Un-huh.

[This statement has no foundation. In all the interviews with the church members, family and friend, all testified to the Roberts' excellent relationship.]

GOODWIN: So when we decided we're going to pick a victim for this kidnapping to pay this loan off, we're going to pick a woman that's having problems with her husband or was it money is the over-riding factor?

LORD: Money is the over-riding factor that that fact was just you knows. . .

GOODWIN: She never gave you any money?

LORD: No.

GOODWIN: Never?

LORD: Never, never.

GOODWIN: We're clear that on August 11th at 10:00 approximately 10:00 A.M. in the morning, that you did go to the home of Doe Roberts and kidnap her with the intent of taking her to your home in Fayette County, Tennessee?

LORD: Yes.

GOODWIN: And therein to restrain her, whatever was necessary, to seek a ransom?

LORD: Yes.

GOODWIN: From Allen Roberts?

LORD: Yes.

LORD: Okay did how much money did she have in her purse?

LORD: About $150.00.

GOODWIN: And you kept that?

LORD: Yes I did.

GOODWIN: When you left there with her in your truck headed to your home, you wasn't 100% sure that she was going to die, but just in case it became necessary, you was prepared?

LORD: Yes I was.

GOODWIN: The straps?

LORD: Yes I was. Well the straps were. . .

GOODWIN: The rags, the chair. . .

LORD: The straps, the straps was to restrain her.

GOODWIN: Where did the chair come from? You made a point of the fact that there was a chair up there. Was it moved from another part of the house?

LORD: It was up in the garage apartment. It was an old chair. The seat wasn't in real. . .

GOODWIN: But it was already there?

LORD: It was already there.

GOODWIN: You didn't have to go get it?

LORD: No.

GOODWIN: Say I got to go get a chair?

LORD: No it was already there.

GOODWIN: Was already there?

LORD: Was already there. It was a wooden chair.

GOODWIN: And the straps were made out of what?

LORD: The straps. I had one old leather belt.

GOODWIN: Un-huh.

LORD: That went around here, around the chair and around the, the, ah, bedrail to keep her from tipping over back and forth, and the other straps were made from, I keep rags out in the, out in the garage, old jumpsuits, old sheets that I usually strip up to tie tomato plants up with, and the I had stripped up a number of those.

GOODWIN: When you buried Mrs. Roberts, you expected if she was ever found that there wouldn't be nothing there?

LORD: That's right.

GOODWIN: But then when you found out the condition that she was in, you knew that we would be able to do an autopsy and isn't that the reason you came back in the second statement when you talked of smothering her and added the sex thing in case we found evidence at the autopsy of sex prior to death?

LORD: Yes that's right. And the reason that I made up in one of the statements too the fact that she came out of the house with a hand full of pills was because I thought that there might be some trace of some kind of pills and everybody would know what she was taking.

GOODWIN: Yeah and that was in the second statement where you didn't remember her purse?

LORD: Yeah that's right.

GOODWIN: You remembered it the first time, in the second one, remember, we didn't, we couldn't remember it at all?

LORD: Well I'm concocting most of these first two anyway and there's. . .

GOODWIN: You know you see, you know, you're so intelligent and you know I look at your background and all and that's why we have a problem with some of this, you understand?

LORD: I understand.

GOODWIN: Because we don't understand you doing that.

LORD: Yeah.

GOODWIN: Unless you can explain it to me?

LORD: I don't, I don't understand it either, I, I don't, I really don't.

GOODWIN: I don't believe that when she left your house that day that she, that you intended for her to come home. I don't believe you could have ever, ever faced her. If you could take all her clothes off, make love to her and all of that business, I don't believe you know, I don't believe she was ever going home, and you don't either.

GOODWIN: I had a slight hope, I really did, that's. . .

LORD: But in the back of your mind, she wasn't coming home and you was prepared?

GOODWIN: In, in, in the back of my mind, I knew that that hope was very slim.

LORD: How much was this loan at the credit union?

LORD: I don't remember. The balance was about $290,000.00.

GOODWIN: And the $290,000.00 loan at the credit union is what drove you to do this and no other reason?

LORD: That's right, that's correct. Well no, not, not entirely because I had a made a couple of bank loans for short periods of time. I just had a lot of things coming due but the thing that was really going to expose me.

GOODWIN: Was that loan there.

LORD: Was that loan there yeah.

GOODWIN: And of course the Roberts had plenty of money and somewhere in there, there was a grudge against the Roberts' wasn't there?

LORD: No sir.

GOODWIN: And that played in picking her?

LORD: No.

GOODWIN: Get even with Allen?

LORD: No sir.

GOODWIN: You could have been real close pals and wouldn't never had a problem?

LORD: No Alan was, you know, I won't, I won't say that I ever liked Alan but, but I didn't dislike him either. Alan, Alan is a, ah, if I can use the word, a peculiar individual, okay. He's not the kind that, he's just not the kind that I would care to get close to. I didn't necessarily like the way he, he treated her in public. Not that it was all that bad but ah he was ah. . .

GOODWIN: It was dark that night you throwed [sic] her in the hole?

LORD: No, it was a full moon.

GOODWIN: Okay, but it was night time?

LORD: Night time.

GOODWIN: Then the next day when you took the leaves off, you're looking at her covered in lime?

LORD: Yeah.

GOODWIN: Can you—and where was her arms at?

LORD: As I remember, they were down by her side.

GOODWIN: Both of them down by her side?

LORD: Yeah.

GOODWIN: Okay and then that's her, both her arms are down by her side and that's when you started finishing the deal, you still think they were down by her side?

LORD: Yeah I, I tried not to look in there too much. I didn't want to look at her. To the best of my recollection, her arms were still by her side.

GOODWIN: Sheriff Kelley, do you have anything to ask him?

KELLEY: No I don't think so Ronnie, you covered everything pretty good.

GOODWIN: Capt. Riles?

RILES: No sir.

GOODWIN: Chief Smith?

MILLS: Chief Mills, no

GOODWIN: Oh I'm sorry; do you have anything you want to ask him for clarity reasons on anything you've heard?

McDANIEL: No I don't have any questions.

GOODWIN: Okay. Mr. Lord, do you have anything to add to the statement?

LORD: Only that I don't know what happened to me. Ah, I don't have a violent history and you just can't believe how I feel.

GOODWIN: But Mr. Lord, you realize. that you kidnapped Doe Roberts?

LORD: Yes sir.

GOODWIN: And that you murdered Doe Roberts?

LORD: No sir that's the truth. And that has been a, ah, a nightmare ever since.

GOODWIN: In the when you never, during the course of this statement which is the truth, there was never, you never did consider taking her to the river?

LORD: No.

GOODWIN: It never played any part in it?

LORD: No.

GOODWIN: You knew we wouldn't find her purse in the river?

LORD: I knew you wouldn't find anything in the river.

GOODWIN: Right. And you didn't want us to. You would point out the body in your own backyard but you wouldn't tell us about the purse?

LORD: That's true.

GOODWIN: Is it, can you tell us why, specifically why? Trinkets strung up and down Seward Road between Shelby County and Fayette County as opposed to an almost complete, her almost complete body, including all her hair as a matter of fact, in your planted in your back yard?

LORD: No I, I can't tell you. I, I, I don't know.

GOODWIN: Chief, is that it? Of course, you know we don't want to leave, ah, we don't want to leave too quickly. I asked you if you had anything to add but I, I can't help but wonder—1984 you joined the church, you basically started knowing Mrs. Roberts in 1984. Were you in love with her or, you done said you didn't hate her. We've cleared that up, right?

LORD: Right.

GOODWIN: Did you love her ah. . .

LORD: I had a great deal of respect for Doe. Ah, one, one winter or spring when my wife was sick when I, when I was working for example, she came over one day because my wife told me and, ah, brought, I think, hot soup for lunch.

214

Ah, no I didn't, I didn't hate Doe Roberts and I wasn't in love with her. Ah, Doe was a fine person.

MILLS: Mr. Lord, I'm Ray Mills with the Sheriff's Office.

LORD: Yes sir.

MILLS: Listen very carefully to me and answer me to the best of your ability. When is this statement going to change?

LORD: Never, never. This is the truth.

MILLS: What can you tell us to make us believe that this is the truth?

LORD: I don't know what I can tell you except this is the truth. You see what I've been trying to do. . .

MILLS: But you said you said that you took her into your apartment, that you set her in a chair, and you tied her legs and feet.

LORD: And around her belly.

MILLS: And around her belly. And you expect us to believe that after we've exhumed her body in the condition that her body was in, you expect us to believe that?

LORD: I guess the only way that I can prove that, Chief Mills, is with the polygraph and I'll be glad to do that.

[Lord pauses briefly, then resumes.]

LORD: No sir that won't happen, that won't happen. See I thought I could beat the polygraph the first time around.

MILLS: Mr. Lord, do you think you can beat this?

LORD: No sir.

MILLS: We sat in here earlier, you, and your attorney, and myself discussed this, that you cannot lie to us. We will eventually find out the truth· This statement you gave today, is it a truth or is it a lie and you think very carefully, is it the truth or is it a lie in this statement?

LORD: It's the truth and the whole truth.

GOODWIN: The only error in the statement would be that when she left her house in your truck, she was never going home? That we done got it down to just a little bit now just a little bit of hope, she was not going home, she was on her way to her grave when she left her home?

LORD: That's the way it turned out and I'll tell you one more time. In my mind, there was a little bit of hope.

MILLS: Why did you dig the grave in your backyard two weeks prior and measured it knowing that you was going to go pick her up? You dug that grave because you knew when you left her house you were going to put her in that grave.

LORD: I thought that was a very high probability.

MILLS: I don't have anything further.

GOODWIN: That concludes the, excuse me, Sheriff Kelly?

KELLY: Mr. Lord, is there anything left at the house that belongs to Doe Roberts?

LORD: No sir.

KELLY: Anything in the apartment?

LORD: No sir.

KELLY: The ties, the tape, and the belt?

LORD: No sir.

KELLY: None of this stuff is there?

LORD: No. The belt buckle may be down there in the burning pile ah but other than that, no sir, there's nothing there.

KELLY: Did you toss the stuff out on the side of the road? Just toss it, driving down the road?

LORD: Un-huh.

GOODWIN: Have you slept in that apartment since this happened?

LORD: I haven't but, but the children have been. My son and his wife from Louisburg have been here two or three times, ah, and they've, they've slept up there. And other than my wife maybe cleaning up before they would come, ah, that's been about it.

GOODWIN: So the covers have been changed?

LORD: Uhmm, probably. You'll have to ask her about that. I don't know. Knowing her, she probably, yeah, she would clean up and wash the sheets and dust and all that stuff before they would come.

GOODWIN: That concludes this statement, what time, 4:45, 4:45 P.M.

CHAPTER SEVENTEEN

Allen

Through the months following Doe's disappearance, the Johnsons, Mary Linda Rose and Ann Richmond would call from time to time and say they missed me at church. Mike Coward would also call me about the Men's Club meetings. Sometimes I would go, but the truth was I just didn't feel comfortable there anymore. During that time I watched most of the congregation change from supporting friends to suspicious associates. Only a precious few remained loyal and convinced of my innocence.

Doe and I had given generously of our time and money to the church that had been our spiritual home since shortly after we moved to Eads. Its members had been foremost among our circle of friends. Apart from square dancing, most of our social life had been focused on the church.

For the first four months after I lost Doe it seemed, apart from family, the congregation stood behind me. But, once I resumed square dancing, things changed. That meeting at Mike Coward's office made me painfully aware that sentiments had changed. Charles Lord had poisoned the minds and hearts of most of the congregation, converting them from sympathy to suspicion. Where they once viewed me as a victim, they then saw me as the perpetrator.

Few things were more discouraging than to walk into the place that had been my spiritual home for over a decade only to experience faces, which used to beam with smiles of welcome, turn away as though ashamed to acknowledge my presence. It sickened me when I would take my customary seat in the pew Doe and I had shared for so many years, only to hear whispers buzzing behind me that could only have to do with one thing. Handshakes that had once been firm and warm now seemed cold and limp.

Charles Lord's arrest and confession brought all this to a head for me. The following Sunday, right before the service was to begin, I stood to address the congregation and said, "I hereby withdraw my membership and support from the Eads United Methodist Church. Take my name from the membership list, as I resign at this time." All kinds of emotions filled me: anger, righteous indignation, resentment at feeling betrayed.

I extended my right arm and pointed at the members, one by one, carefully omitting those who had remained steadfast and loyal to me—Carl and Karen Johnson, Ronald Cline, the Richmonds, and perhaps a few others, and told them, "I've watched as you've gone from being my supporters to my accusers. You lost faith in me and my innocence. There is nothing to keep me here now." It was all I could do to keep my words civil and to refrain from using profane expletives to express my true feelings.

The loyal few tried with loving words to make me change my mind, but there was no turning back. I walked out the door of the Eads United Methodist Church and have not returned.

Mary Linda Rose

Looking back now I can see Charles and Sylvia sitting up there on the front row with their grandchildren, keeping up their pretense. No wonder Allen didn't feel comfortable! I'll never forget that terrible day Allen resigned from the church.

I remember so well how, on September 5, 1993, Allen stood up from his customary pew at the back of the church and asked that his name be removed from the membership. He pointed an accusing finger at the many individuals whom he felt had been seduced by Charles Lord and abandoned him, carefully omitting us, the Johnsons, and Mr. Cline. This was the Sunday before the Tuesday of Doe's funeral. Mother and I immediately got up and went over to him, saying, "Allen, no. Please don't do this. Don't leave our church family. We love you and want you to stay."

Allen looked around at all the others who had remained in their seats. I stared at everyone, pleading silently for more support.

Mike Coward spoke up, "Allen, please don't do this now. Please give it some time."

Shaking his head emphatically, he responded, "No, I can't do that."

Hazel Richmond

It was like a dagger went through my heart that day, but I can understand why he did what he did.

Mary Linda Rose

Allen just turned and went out the door. I thought to myself, if we have failed anybody, we have failed this man from the word "go." That was an awful day.

Family and Friends

Allen and Doe's family could not understand why Doe's body wasn't released to them. The autopsy had been performed on Thursday, September 1st. Yet the family was still waiting. Allen had called several times and was told that they could not release the body. Willie's daughter, Marti Eason, who is a nurse, finally was able to contact the Medical Examiner's Office sometime during the weekend, and asked if they had finished the autopsy and all their extensive testing. When she was told that all had been done, she asked point-blank, "Then you have no good reason to withhold the body from her family. This family needs to bury her!"

* * *

From *The Commercial Appeal,* September 8, 1993:

EULOGY RECALLS DOE ROBERTS AS SELF-SACRIFICING

Source: William Thomas

Kidnap victim Martha 'Doe' Roberts was eulogized Tuesday as a kind, generous woman who bought groceries for strangers, took toys to sick children, and loved her husband and square dancing. "She was always doing things for somebody else," recalled Rev. Bill Sawtell, a longtime friend, who preached at the funeral service before 400 to 500 people exactly 13 months after Roberts disappeared from her Eads home.

Her remains, which were found last week in the backyard of neighbor-suspect Charles Lord, were buried in Memorial Park Cemetery in a red casket covered with red roses.

More than half the mourners who filled the Memorial Park chapel were square dancers whom Roberts and her husband, Allen, had met during more than 30 years of dance activity.

In addition, eight long pews were filled with family and relatives, including some of the nieces and nephews the couple took in and sent to school. At one time, said Sawtell, four nieces and nephews were living with the Roberts.

For a year, none of the family knew if Doe Roberts was dead or alive. "It's been very hard," said Jewell Knox, a sister. "But now at least we know what happened. When we get her put away today, I'll do better."

Six framed photographs of Doe Roberts, who would have been 66, were on display at either end of the casket. They were photographs of a pleasant-looking woman whom Sawtell said will be missed.

"She took toys to children at St. Jude's (Children's Research Center) and she was the square dancer who was always there to help straighten things out. If she saw someone at the grocery store start to put something back because they couldn't afford it, she'd tell them to keep it, she'd pay for it. She bought a lot of groceries for people."

Roberts and her husband had been married since 1948, and people at the funeral said they were always together. In a memorial, Allen Roberts wrote, "we were seldom apart; she fed me, clothed me, and told me when to get a haircut."

At the graveside, Roberts lingered for an hour, talking with crowds of friends who gathered around him after the service.

In the final prayer, Sawtell asked for divine help in understanding why bad things happen to good people.

Family and Friends

Allen picked out a brilliant red casket for Doe. "It was the most beautiful casket I had ever seen," remembers Hazel Richmond.

Malinda Lancaster also went to the funeral. She and her husband moved to Florida a few weeks later. Malinda says, "Our move wasn't connected to Doe's death, but we were glad to be away from Great Oaks."

Esther Hammons

Because of our misgivings about the Eads United Methodist Church, its minister, and many in its congregation, Allen arranged for Doe's funeral to be held at Memorial Park Funeral Home in Memphis. The service was simple and sweet, with many who had known and loved Doe speaking their final thoughts of farewell for her. Foremost, of course, was Allen.

The Sentencing Hearing

Allen

On October 19, 1993, Charles Lord appeared before Tennessee Circuit Court Judge Kerry Blackwood, who sentenced him to life in prison for the murder of my wife. All Lord's cunning finally caught up with him at that moment because, in addition, the judge sentenced him to the maximum penalty for rape in the state of Tennessee, twenty years. The sentences were to be served consecutively. This effectively assured that Lord would never leave prison alive.

Judge Blackwood told Lord, in passing sentence, "You are a dangerous offender. . . with little or no regard for human life. My prayer. . . is that the community can go back and put their lives back together."

Karen Johnson

I wouldn't have gone to the Somerville courthouse if Miriam hadn't called me. The courthouse sits in the town square, skirted by large oaks shading the sidewalks and benches. Out front, the TV film crews created a disturbance at odds with the stately setting. Miriam and I made our way up the wide marble steps to the courtroom on the second floor.

We had sat for only a few minutes when Sylvia and one of the Lords' daughters came in. Miriam said, "Karen, we need to go over and speak to Sylvia. She's still one of our church members and we need to act like Christians."

We stood up, walked over to Sylvia, and spoke, but Sylvia wouldn't even look at us. After a moment, Miriam and I returned to our seats.

I remember sitting there looking at Charles, thinking about how he had killed my friend and stolen the church's money. How could he?

Miriam Foley

Karen Johnson and I went to the court house in Somerville together. We had not seen or talked to Sylvia Lord since before Charles was arrested. As we were sitting there, I told Karen that we were still members of the church and, as such, we should say something to Sylvia and Andrea, the Lords' youngest daughter.

We stood and went over to where Sylvia and Andrea were sitting.

"Sylvia, how are you?" I asked. But Sylvia would not look at nor speak to me and Karen at all.

I persisted, "Sylvia, have you decided not to talk to us anymore?"

She did not reply, so Karen and I went back to our seats. We haven't heard from or seen Sylvia since then.

Allen Roberts

Bill was the one who escorted me to both court appearances, where Lord entered his guilty plea and then when Lord was sentenced. Bill drove me to Somerville, knowing I needed his presence for support. We sat together in the courtroom for the sentencing hearing, with Bill at the end of the pew. I noticed William Paul Knox had seated himself immediately behind Bill.

Just before Lord was brought in, one deputy approached another who was standing in the middle of the aisle. They talked briefly and then one who had been standing near us came and took a position next to William Paul and Bill, placing himself between the two of them and the aisle. It was obvious the deputies anticipated trouble.

When the guards brought Lord in, they came down that same aisle. I know if Bill could have gotten his hands on Lord, he would have saved the taxpayers a lot of money, but we were all bound by the law and the criminal justice system.

After the judge finished pronouncing sentence and Lord was escorted out, I broke down and wept.

The Congregation

The Church members wrestled with this terrible revelation, this betrayal of trust. Some found it difficult to believe that Charles Lord, whom they had trusted, and who had been foremost in providing spiritual and emotional support to them throughout this year, was guilty.

"How could he? Why would he?" So began a questioning, discussing, and soul searching that continues to this day.

Ann Richmond

Sometime in September, after Charles was arrested, I was talking to Carl Johnson one day. We were discussing details of the case and I asked him if he had called Sylvia the night I got my call from the kidnapper.

"No, I didn't," Carl told me.

I fault the FBI for not getting back in touch. Maybe, if they had, we would have put the pieces together. You know we say a lot of "ifs" now. . . *if we had all just gotten together and talked.*

We also have pictures of the church children sitting in the backyard at Charles and Sylvia's house in August, less than two weeks after Doe disappeared. Sitting right there, just a few feet from where Doe was buried!

Our Scholarship Fund was established about the time the Lords join the church. It was done in honor of Olivia Anderson, the mother of a member. Through the years a number of children in the church applied for and received $500 a semester if their grades were in good standing. The first year my oldest granddaughter became eligible for it, she had to submit her records to Charles for his approval. She received the scholarship for two semesters, but the next time she applied, Charles said that the fund was running mighty short.

I just couldn't believe the fund was that low. The last report I had indicated there was plenty of money. I wondered about it at the time, but didn't say anything. Charles had been the head financial officer at the Defense Depot. He let us know that he was used to handling millions of dollars on a daily basis, and would be glad to take care of the church.

In a small church, anyone who is willing to take a job is going to get it. We passed responsibilities around, but if someone wanted to keep on with a job—well, we would just let them. Charles and Sylvia were real workers in the church and we never questioned that fact. Now, of course, we know Charles cleaned that Scholarship account out in June before he took Doe in August.

Gus Richmond

Two or three days after Doe disappeared, I dreamed about her. I was sitting in my chair like I always do, watching TV, and dozed off. I dreamed I looked her in the face just as close to me as you sitting right there. She was lying in a grave.

I woke up hollering. I thought I knew just where the grave was. When I drove to what I thought was the site, though, I didn't find anything, so I never told anyone but Ann about the dream.

Mary Linda Rose

Jo Anne and Ramona came to meet with us at the church in the weeks immediately following Doe's funeral. We had our service as usual and then at the end here they came. We sat back down and they began telling us that they had Charles and all the rest.

I got angry and I'm still angry about a lot of things. I demanded, "What are you doing here today?"

"Well, the case is still open," Jo Anne answered.

"What do you mean the case is 'still open'? You have Charles!"

Jo Anne then started to answer a question from someone else, but I interrupted her, saying, "Wait a minute. Are you telling me that you are now looking for somebody else?"

Jo Anne just looked at me and said, "Yes."

"Are you telling us there is somebody else sitting in this congregation today who had some responsibility in Doe's disappearance?"

Jo Anne said quickly and sort of quiet, "I don't want to talk to you."

That made me angry. I said, "You will talk to me! You tell me what's going on. Is there somebody here we should be worried about?"

Jo Anne just said, "Don't get comfortable."

"Well isn't that just great. You haven't told me anything!"

After that, Mother and I went to church together every Sunday and, each time, I carried a pistol in my big purse. When I wasn't playing, my hand was in the purse on the gun. Whenever I got up to play the piano, Mother would stick her hand in the purse. Now isn't that a great way to go to church?

I am still angry. It has taken me a long time to figure out what all my anger was about. Early on, we went to Reverend DeBardeleban for help. We said, "We're angry and frightened and need help." Nothing ever transpired. We contacted the Superintendent of our Methodist district and his response was, "What do you need?"

We said, "We don't know what we need. We're hurting. There's someone in our church who has disappeared. There's problems. Big problems. Maybe we need some counselors."

Nobody ever came. It was like we were out there all alone. DeBardeleban wouldn't or probably couldn't help. He was so close to Charles and Sylvia, and as manipulated by them as we were. He was never, ever able to step out of his role as a human being and minister to someone else in need. Years before, we had had a minister, Reverend King, who was a Rock of Gibraltar. I wanted Brother Jim DeBardeleban to be like Reverend King.

Hazel Richmond

I find it so hard to know what to believe about Sylvia. I don't know how a woman could be married to someone who did those things and not suspect anything. Yet I do know that after Charles was arrested, Sylvia went to a neighbor for help in balancing her own check book. I also remember once, long before Charles was arrested, I went with her, at her request, to help pick out something to wear to a family reunion. Sylvia tried on a number of dresses and, when she was ready to pay, she first called Charles. She explained what she was doing. Then, and only then, did she go and put the clothes on a charge card. That seemed so peculiar to me, how Charles had such control over her.

Another Perspective on Charles Lord

After everything came out, Mike Coward was appointed to the board of a local private school. He walked into the meeting room and saw on the wall a picture of one of the Lords' children. When he asked about it, they told him what a problem Charles had been. There had been numerous times when his checks were returned and other times when Charles was angry and made threatening calls on the phone to staff members. This was a very different Charles Lord from the one the Cowards had known at church.

Carl and Karen Johnson

Even before Doe was taken, many in the church thought we needed a new pastor. Charles was on the Pastor and Parish Committee and told us that we didn't have a say. We felt that, if 54 people wanted a change and the six on the committee didn't, the change should be made. Now, looking back, I can see that Charles was afraid of what might be discovered if there was a change.

We didn't even know that the church had those funds Lord took. That didn't matter as long as the church paid its bills. We can't understand how Charles was able to take the money as he hadn't been a signatory on the accounts. No one had made that change since Mike Richmond died. We just don't understand how Charles convinced the Peoples Bank in Collierville to let him withdraw those funds.

Brother Nance was pastor when we started the Scholarship Fund. He would give us reports on how much was in it every time we had a church business meeting.

Malinda Lancaster

Charles bragged about how well they were doing when he retired. They bought a Cadillac that same year and did some remodeling, but I never saw any indications of lavish spending. Sylvia liked to sew and made all of her own clothes.

I tried to be cooperative with the FBI. I called Jo Anne several times, but they never told us anything about the case. I was floored when Charles was arrested.

Afterwards, Ramona told me that the case was still open. There were several questions that had never been answered, such as what happened to the money. This didn't make me anxious, but I sure was curious.

I went to all the court appearances, but Sylvia never spoke to me. She just glared at us, like we were aliens or something. I did not even try to visit Sylvia after Charles was arrested. I didn't want to know any more about her.

I saw Allen several times at court, but he never spoke to me. He doesn't like me now. I told Allen I was sorry, that I was a victim of the situation as much as he was, but he wouldn't speak to me or look at me. He was really upset because I thought he did it. Once, Lon and I ran into Allen at Kroger. Allen turned and left the store rather than speak. It was obvious he didn't want to speak to me. I am sorry he feels that way, but I was drawn into this thing and believe I wasn't responsible.

I went to the courthouse in Somerville with Miriam and some others. The sentencing hearing was conducted upstairs in the larger court room. We all thought Charles should have gotten the death penalty.

We had little contact with Charles and Sylvia before they joined the church. They were the kind who would only speak if you knocked them down. Sylvia was hard to get to know. I didn't know her at all until we got the Extension Club going in 1985. I really felt that the Lords thought they were better than anyone else—they acted as though they were higher up the social ladder than we were.

After this was all over, I thought to myself many times, I've been to the same altar and knelt at communion many times with this man who murdered my friend and buried her in his own back yard.

Doe tried to be Sylvia's friend. When we all went to Pigeon Forge for the Extension Club convention, Sylvia and Doe roomed together. Sylvia complained later that she would never room with Doe again because Doe snored.

I feel sorry for Sylvia in a way, but it's hard not to think that she didn't know anything about all this.

Doe was such a sweet person and wanted friends. She would do anything for you. She'd give you the shirt off her back. She would call me and say, "Come pick some of these turnip greens, Malinda. I've got all I need in the freezer."

She would show up on my door step with flowers, thrift and what have you, to plant in my yard. We were all trying to get things to grow in our yards. She made an afghan for me. She was always giving people things. I appreciated it. She was my friend and I was her friend.

After Doe disappeared, I was always looking for her. Even now, after we moved to Florida, sometimes I see some woman from the back and for a moment think, "There's Doe!"

I could never imagine Charles as a killer. I never saw him being violent. He could be brusque and rude, but Charles was so sympathetic to Hazel Richmond after her husband Mike died. Hazel, like me after my mother died, would get so upset when we started singing the hymns. She was having a hard time and Charles was the Finance Steward. I'm sure she turned a lot of things over to him about that time, but Hazel is such an honorable person—she would never have given him outright any of the church's money.

Agent Jo Anne Overall and Inspector Ramona Swain

Inspector Ramona Swain and Agent Jo Anne Overall differed from the beginning of the case about Allen Roberts. Swain always felt, and even now still feels, Allen was guilty, but Overall never did. Agent Overall followed agency protocol, yet, in her heart she believed Allen Roberts was also a victim, never a perpetrator.

What people do not realize is that Charles Lord came to the investigators in January of 1993, offering to help them solve the case, telling them he had been contacted by the kidnapper. They, as professional law enforcement officers, were required to follow all leads, yet it seemed from the beginning there was something wrong with what Charles was telling them. His statements simply did not ring true, yet they had just enough of a smattering of truth in them that the investigators could not rule them out.

Whenever they planned and worked with Lord, something inevitably went wrong. They would set up surveillance equipment when he told them the kidnapper had phoned him and arranged a "drop" at his mailbox. Then, right before the "drop" occurred, the equipment would mysteriously fail, apparently from someone having tampered with it.

The same thing happened with any wiretaps on the Lords' telephones. Shortly before any calls from the kidnapper to the Lords, the monitors would mysteriously fail to function.

All of these factors aroused their suspicions about Charles Lord, culminating in their investigation of his finances and those of the Eads United Methodist Church.

Retrospective

The net of evil worked by Charles Lord stretched over the entire community of Eads, Tennessee. Even though the little Methodist church is still in existence, its congregation is only a fraction of what it was before the abduction and murder of Doe Roberts. Its members still attend and pray, but the flame that Doe and Allen had faithfully tended has all but sputtered out.

There are a number of theories about what Lord's motives were and how and why he acted on them. In retrospect it seems the ransom he demanded was too little and too late to save him from his financial downfall. Instead, it appears he knew Doe was the one who had discovered the financial irregularities at the church and Lord felt compelled to silence her. With her propensity for kindness and belief that people are basically good, it appears she might have contacted Charles Lord and let him know she was aware, but gave him one final chance to return the money. The fact that he had already dissipated the funds left him only one course of action—to kill Doe.

In January of 1994, Lord was sentenced in federal court to serve ten years and five months for his financial crimes, with the sentence to run concurrent with his sentence for the abduction and murder of Doe Roberts.

Lord's crime against Doe apparently made such a deep impression on Judge Blackwood that, in February of 1994, he announced that he would no longer allow plea bargaining in his court—no negotiated sentences. Accused criminals appearing in his court would only have two choices: either plead guilty or no contest to the charges or go to trial.

Larry Knox, Doe's nephew, claimed and received from Allen the $25,000 reward he had offered for information leading to Doe.

Inspector Ramona Swain, who steadfastly believed Allen Roberts was guilty and at first refused even to consider the Knox brothers' accusations of Charles Lord, received the Deputy of the Month Award from the Shelby County Sheriff's Department for the month of November, 1993, in recognition of her work on the Doe Roberts case. In nominating her, Captain J. P. Tucker wrote, ". . . Through her sense of dedication and perseverance, this mystery was solved."

Sylvia Lord divorced her husband, but not in the traditional sense. She took marital property before the creditors he had defrauded could attach it and obtained a "Divorce from Bed and Board," or what some people claim is a legal separation. It allowed her to receive his lucrative government pension, which she never would have obtained from an absolute divorce.

Even now she is reported to pay him regular visits at the Turney Correctional Center where he is incarcerated.

CHAPTER EIGHTEEN

Esther Roberts

As tragic as Doe's fate was, knowing at last what had happened to her brought Allen closure. With Allen no longer under suspicion, our relief was beyond measure. Finally, we were able to get back to living normal lives. The home Allen promised me was finished in the spring of 1994, and on May 26, we married.

Our home sits on a two acre tract where we grow vegetables and have planted lots of flowers which draw all kinds of birds to our yard. Allen continues to be an avid bird watcher.

In 1999, five years after we married, Allen presented me with an adorable, solid white female Maltese puppy. We named this nine pound dynamo "Sugar." She is a delight to us. Since Allen is childless and mine are grown, this loving little dog is for all practical purposes our "daughter."

My family loves Allen and living next door has not caused any problems because we are so close in spirit. They are extremely happy that I have found someone who truly loves me and is so good to me and all my loved ones.

Allen

When I look back upon those thirteen months Doe was missing and think of all the suffering so many others including me endured because of our fatal friendship with Charles Lord, I sometimes wonder how God could allow such things to happen. Then I look around at my present situation, knowing I once more have a loving, devoted wife and life partner; knowing Charles Lord will never know freedom and will pay for what he did the rest of his life; and I feel some sense of justice and justness.

The *Book of Job* in the Holy Bible tells of a righteous man who had everything he loved and valued taken from him. Despite his deprivations and many sorrows, Job never relinquished his faith in God. In the end, God rewarded Job many times over for keeping his faith.

I do not claim to be righteous like Job. However, like him, I found myself struggling many times during that terrible ordeal to hold on to my faith. In November of 1992, standing in the apple orchard, I asked God what to do. The answer which came to me was both simple and profound, what would Doe want me to do?

That sent me back to Top Spinners, where I found Esther. I shall always feel that I was directed by God and by Doe's loving spirit to return to square dancing so Esther and I could find each other and she could help me through my plight. She, too, is a person of faith.

As always, there were those who judged prematurely and cast aspersions, criticism, accusations, and doubt upon me. The whole ordeal of losing Doe taught me how imperfect man's justice and understanding are. But family, friends, religious faith, and holding fast to your own principles can see you through almost anything. I tried my best to follow both my heart and my head. I also kept my faith. Like Job at the end of his book, I feel God has rewarded me.

Finis